The Cut-flower
Garden

. . .

The Cut-flower Garden

. . .

Theodore James, Jr.

Photography by Harry Haralambou

Macmillan Publishing Company
New York

Maxwell Macmillan Canada
Toronto

Maxwell Macmillan International
New York   Oxford   Singapore   Sydney

Frontispiece: This simple arrangement of kerria, grape hyacinths, yellow-and-green euphorbia, and deep blue anemones, either homegrown or florist-purchased, is an utter knockout. Arrangement by Alix Ehlers; cream pitcher by Arizona potter Toni Sodersten.

Copyright © 1993 by Theodore James, Jr.
Photography copyright © 1993 by Harry Haralambou

All rights reserved. No part of this book may be reproduced or transmitted in any form or by any means, electronic or mechanical, including photocopying, recording, or by any information storage and retrieval system, without permission in writing from the Publisher.

Macmillan Publishing Company
866 Third Avenue
New York, NY 10022

Maxwell Macmillan Canada, Inc.
1200 Eglinton Avenue East, Suite 200
Don Mills, Ontario M3C 3N1

Macmillan Publishing Company is part of the Maxwell Communication Group of Companies.

Library of Congress Cataloging-in-Publication Data

James, Theodore.
The cut-flower garden / Theodore James, Jr. ;
photography by Harry Haralambou.
p.   cm.
Includes index.
ISBN 0-02-558912-1
1. Flower arrangement.   2. Cut flowers.   3. Flowers.
4. Flower gardening.   5. Landscape gardening.   I. Title.
SB449.J33   1993
745.92—dc20   92-27310
CIP

Macmillan books are available at special discounts for bulk purchases for sales promotions, premiums, fund-raising, or educational use. For details, contact:

Special Sales Director
Macmillan Publishing Company
866 Third Avenue
New York, NY 10022

10   9   8   7   6   5   4   3   2   1

PRINTED IN THE UNITED STATES OF AMERICA

To Ellen

With many thanks for your kind interest and help.

Here, the arranger has taken a simple bouquet of annual pinks and placed them in a round form arrangement. This shape arrangement is particularly useful as a table center-piece. Arrangement by Fleurette Guiloz.

Contents

· · ·

Acknowledgments

. . .

We are grateful to the following friends and neighbors who so graciously contributed their time and talents in creating lovely flower arrangements for us: Ellen Kosciusko, Helga Dawn, Jane Overman, Barbara Woodward, Alix Ehlers, Irene Moran, Robert A. Schaefer, Jr., Lucille Siracusano of Feather Hill Country Flowers, Southold, New York, Jacqueline Penney, Mable Brown, Darlene Cichanowicz, Madame Walda Poiron, and Fleurette Guiloz.

We would also like to thank the following who allowed us to photograph the arrangements in their homes: Dorothy Lueckoff, Roberta Lee, Marietta Silvestre, Pat and Bill Milford, Fran George.

Also Mrs. Farmer Mike, Cutchogue, New York, who generously contributed cut flowers; Ellen Talmage of Friar's Head Farm, Riverhead, New York; Peter Prescott; L. Herndon Werth; Alice Levien; landscape designer Connie Cross, Cutchogue, New York; Caroline T. Kiang of the Suffolk County, New York, Cooperative Extension; Toni Sadersten, American Hand and Classic Porcelains, New York City, New York.

Also the Netherlands Flower Bulb Information Center; Monrovia Nursery Co.; Jackson & Perkins; Thompson and Morgan; White Flower Farm; Musser Forests, Inc.; Bluestone Perennials; Niche Gardens; Klehm Nursey; Doroski's Nursery, Inc.; Ging's Nursery, Inc.; and Gardener's Supply Co.

Also, Mrs. Carleton Cole, our agent; our editor, Pam Hoenig; and our editor's assistant, Justin Schwartz.

Here, flowering dogwood, kerria, and wisteria blossoms have been turned into a lovely, harmonious outdoor centerpiece. Notice that the arrangement is in the form of an asymmetrical triangle, particularly suited to loose-flowered creations. Arrangement by Alix Ehlers.

Introduction

. . .

If you've ever browsed through those upscale magazines about the homes of the rich and famous, you've probably noticed that most of the rooms pictured have extravagant bouquets of flower arrangements all over the place. Live flowers bring life to a room, humanize it, and add the finishing touches to any decor. And, although you may not have a Louis XVI chair, a priceless antique Persian rug, a collection of Georgian silver, or a Picasso on the wall, by simply adding lush bouquets of flowers here and there throughout the house, you'll be surprised how lavish and lovely your house will look.

The Cut-flower Garden is designed to offer not only basic flower arranging instructions and suggestions, but to advise you how to landscape your property so that you will have armfuls of material for lavish cut-flower and dried arrangements all through the year. In other words, if you are selecting shrubs and flowering trees to landscape your property, why not select those that offer material for indoor arrangements? And, if you are installing a garden of bulbs, annuals, perennials, or roses, why not select species and varieties which you can use to decorate the inside of your house as well as the outside?

By studying this book and the suggestions it contains, and by spending a little money and time purchasing and planting, you'll be on your way to learning one of the tricks of upscale decorators and designers. That is, that any room can be made to look extravagant and luxurious with the addition of opulent bouquets of fresh or dried cut flowers and foliage.

We sincerely hope you will find the suggestions here useful and that they will add the dimension of the beauty of flowers to your personal environment and life-style.

How to Use This Book

The Cut-flower Garden is concerned with not only gathering material for and fashioning your own indoor flower arrangements, but with how to grow all of the material necessary for making these arrangements.

The book is divided into several sections. The first is the cut-flower calendar, a month-by-month plan of what to do both in the garden and in creating flower arrangements to enjoy indoors. In this section, you will be referred to more specific information regarding the various projects which are contained in other sections of the book, as well as for proper planting times to assure you have cut-flower material.

Next is a section on the basic techniques of cutting and conditioning cut flowers. Special sections on forcing shrub material and bulbs, as well as on drying follow, then a chapter on the principles of flower arranging. All of the entries on individual plants follow, with relevant growing instructions. At the end there is a section listing sources for planting material which you may wish to avail yourself of.

Read through the calendar and the various individual entries, acquainting yourself with the plants most suited to making cut-flower arrangements and the times of the year when they are available. Naturally you won't want all of the plants included, for there are far too many for the average garden. Look through the lists and decide which are suitable for the kinds of flower arrangements you think you might want to make. Think about what kinds of textures, colors, and scents you like. Also think about your own limitations in terms of time and space available.

Keep in mind that if you have an established landscape, many of the types of flowering trees, shrubs, and dwarf conifers suitable for arrangements may already be on your property.

Then, with these factors in mind, you can start to select the plants you wish to grow.

The Cut-flower
Garden

. . .

This mini-arrangement of snowdrops, Iris reticulata, *and miniature daffodils is sure to lift the spirits during midwinter doldrums.* Arrangement by Lucille Siracusano, Feather Hill Country Flowers and Gifts.

1

The Cut-flower Calendar

. . .

The cut-flower calendar will keep you posted not only on what cutting material you'll be wanting for indoor arrangements, but what chores you should be doing in the garden, and which plants you may wish to add to your cutting garden. In the case of specific plants, you will be referred to extended cultivation entries elsewhere in the book.

January
Arrangements in the house

- There usually are no flowers in the flower garden in January, unless one lives in a mild-winter climate or plants *very* early blooming spring bulbs in the fall in the proper location for earliest bloom, that is, in a sheltered position with a southern exposure, next to a heat-absorbing wall or foundation. (A dark-colored wall is preferred, as it will function as a passive solar storage unit.) Snowdrops (*Galanthus*), and Christmas or Lenten roses (*Helleborus*) may bloom in January in some areas of the country and can be cut for indoor arrangements.

- Evergreen material (conifers and broad-leaved plants, many bearing colorful berries, such as holly and fire thorn) can be cut and used in winter arrangements. See pages 126–133.

- Deciduous shrubs which have colored bark, such as red-twig dogwood, are available for cutting (page 120), as is the one shrub which does bloom as early as January, witch hazel (page 123).
- Bulbs such as crocus, grape hyacinth, and *Iris danfordiae* and *I. reticulata* can be brought out of chilling areas and forced now. See pages 22–24.
- The blooms of winter-flowering houseplants, such as cyclamen, can be cut and used in arrangements.
- Everlastings and silica-dried flower stalks can be used in dried flower arrangements.
- Beyond what is available at home, there is the option of purchasing a few flowers from the florist and adding them to cut material from the garden for arrangements or, by using small plastic water containers inserted into the soil, dressing up houseplants.
- Tender bulbs such as amaryllis, paperwhite narcissus, and prechilled hyacinths, tulips, etc., are still available through mail-order or at garden centers or florists.

What to do in the garden

- Beyond gathering colored bark material, evergreen cuttings, the very early flowering bulbs and witch hazel, the end of January is the time to begin forcing shrub and flowering tree material for February and March. Take cuttings of such things as forsythia and pussy willow (see pages 121–122).
- Plan your garden purchases, as well as garden beds and borders for the rest of the year. Begin planning for the April and May planting of various shrubs, conifers, broad-leaved evergreens, and flowering trees suitable for the cut-flower garden. Visit local garden centers and nurseries and inquire whether or not the plants and seeds you want will be available. If not, check the mail-order sources.

February
Arrangements in the house

- Continue bulb forcing.
- Some shrub material cut in January for forcing should be ready to bloom.
- Nurtured winter-blooming bulbs such as amaryllis should begin to bloom, and can be used in cut arrangements.
- In warmer climates, new, fresh green growth should be appearing on some trees and shrubs to add greenery to arrangements.
- Mini-arrangements of very early blooming spring bulbs, such as *Iris reticulata* and *I. danfordiae*, puschkinia, snowdrops, scilla, crocus, and mini-daffodils, can be put together with forced flowering shrub and tree material, such as forsythia, flowering peach, cherry, plum, and pussy willow.

What to do in the garden

- Continue to plan for the heavy work months ahead in terms of selecting and purchasing material and planning summer and fall gardens.
- Set up an indoor light structure for those tender annuals you'll need to get a head start on (page 43).

March
Arrangements in the house

- By the end of March, in many parts of the country, outdoor cutting material becomes plentiful. Early tulips, daffodils, hyacinths, guinea hen flowers, are all making their appearance.

- In some parts of the country, early spring-blooming perennials such as bleeding heart and violas are beginning to bloom. These can be combined with spring-blooming bulbs.
- Forsythia, pussy willow, and other flowering shrubs and trees are beginning to bloom outdoors in many parts of the country.
- Forced flowering shrub material continues to come into bloom if started in January and February.

What to do in the garden

- Pansies in flats are now available at garden centers and nurseries and can be planted for cut-flower use.
- In warmer areas of the country, it is time to start outdoor planting of annuals (larkspur, bachelor's button, etc.) which endure some chilling.
- Most of the annuals which need an indoor head start under lights should be planted now.
- Prune existing rose plantings (page 109).
- Fertilize existing plantings.
- It is time to install many early-blooming perennials.
- The pruning of some shrubs and flowering trees is in order. Check individual entries for specific information. The pruned material can be used in arrangements.
- Prepare beds for later spring planting (page 45).
- Install some shrubs and flowering trees (pages 115–117).

April
Arrangements in the house

- By April, the outdoor spring garden should be in full swing, with daffodils, early tulips, hyacinths, and grape hyacinth all in bloom, so there is no need to resort to forcing, houseplant material, or purchased flowers in arrangements.
- Early-blooming perennials continue to bloom in the southern areas of the country and begin to bloom farther north.
- In some parts of the country early azaleas and other broad-leaved evergreens, as well as some deciduous shrubs, are beginning to bloom.

What to do in the garden

- By the end of the month, in the colder areas of the country, sow seeds of the hardier annuals (larkspur, bachelor's button, calendula) in the garden to provide annual bloom for the summer months (page 46).
- It is time to select and plant new shrubs, flowering trees, and evergreens (pages 115–117). Don't forget to purchase some holly bushes for cuttings this Christmas (page 130).
- Plant chrysanthemums for fall cutting material. Pinch the tips of each shoot every two weeks until July 4 to promote bushiness and more bloom (page 86).
- All annuals which need a head start under lights should be planted by now.
- Select and plant rosebushes for cutting throughout the coming season (pages 107–109).
- Select and plant perennials (pages 80–81).

In this May arrangement, cherry-colored tulips combine well with pink dogwood, weigela, and white lilac. Arrangement by Irene Moran.

May

Arrangements in the house

- Late tulips and daffodils are still in bloom.
- Biennials, such as Canterbury bells (*Campanula medium*), delphiniums, sweet William, and foxglove, are in bloom.
- Many perennials are in bloom now, including peonies, poppies, and astilbe.
- Azaleas are now in bloom farther north. These can all be put to good use in arrangements for the house.

What to do in the garden

- Outdoors sow the seeds of the tender annuals such as cosmos, nasturtiums, marigolds, zinnias, etc., which will be used for cutting during the summer. See page 46.

- Continue setting out flowering shrubs, roses, and trees as well as evergreens.
- Continue to install new perennial plantings.
- Sow seeds of everlastings for use in fall and winter dried arrangements (pages 54–56).
- Install various ornamental grasses to use dried in fall and winter arrangements (pages 103–105).
- Purchase six-packs of asters and plant them, as they bloom in October and can be used for arrangements then. Do not plant them in the same place two years in a row since diseases which attack asters may remain in surrounding soil over the winter.
- Plant silver-foliaged plants such as artemisia, lavender cotton, and dusty miller for drying in fall and use in Christmas arrangements.
- Plant tender bulbs such as dahlias and gladiolus, as well as hardy lilies, and others for cut-flower use in August and September.

Pale blue delphiniums and coralbells soften the look of the flamboyant deep pink double peonies. Arrangement by Irene Moran.

June

Arrangements in the house

- Gather perennials and roses which are in bloom for lush indoor arrangements.
- Toward the end of the month, annuals planted in May will begin to bloom and be available for arrangements.

What to do in the garden

- Weed, water, and care for annuals planted in April and May.

- Cut delphiniums and othere perennial favorites for silica drying, so that dried flowers will be available during the winter for arrangements. See pages 30–31.

July

Arrangements in the house

- Although the first flush of rose bloom is over, they will bloom sporadically through the summer.
- Much annual and perennial cut-flower material continues to be available. Early-blooming lilies will also be available.

Roses are so utilitarian in the cut-flower garden, because like the hybrid tea 'Fascination' pictured here, they bloom all through the summer and well into the fall.

What to do in the garden

- Continue to weed, water, and care for annuals, as well as other plants in the garden.
- Continue to cut and silica dry favorite flowers for winter arrangements.

August
Arrangements in the house

- Annuals continue to be available in great quantities. Use them throughout the house.
- Tender bulbs such as gladiolus and dahlias are at their best now and in September.
- Take a stroll out into the country and gather wildflowers such as goldenrod, wild aster, and Queen Anne's lace for arrangements and drying.

What to do in the garden

- Sow the seeds of biennials such as foxglove, sweet William, delphinium, and Canterbury bells (*Campanula medium*) each year to keep a constant stock for use in late April and May, when they bloom. Check individual entries for specific information.
- Plant Siberian iris and peonies now for use in May and June when they bloom.
- Do not plant shrubs and trees yet, as they are still putting forth seasonal growth, and do not transplant well under these circumstances. Wait until next month to begin this.
- If you didn't plant chrysanthemums in spring, purchase plants from garden centers and nurseries and install them now for October and November cutting material.

September
Arrangements in the house

- Continue using summer annuals and late-blooming perennials for arrangements.
- The second flush of rose bloom, often more beautiful than the June bloom, is ready for cutting now.
- Continue gathering wild material for drying. Plants with pods such as milkweed, as well as rushes and cattails, are now at their prime for drying.

What to do in the garden

- Start planting flowering shrubs such as forsythia, pussy willow, flowering crab apple, cherry, peach, and plum for forcing in January and for garden cutting material in April and May. See pages 115–117.

October
Arrangements in the house

- Perennial chrysanthemums are in bloom now and are a welcome change from the summer flowers of August and September. Various dried grasses add nice autumn touches to arrangements.
- Continue to gather pods and dried material from the wild. The pods of Siberian iris are particularly attractive in both live and dried arrangements.

What to do in the garden

- Sow larkspur seeds now, as they winter over and will provide striking material for use in May (page 50).

This drift of pink chrysanthemums with Japanese red maples in the distance offers not only an eyeful of beauty in the autumn landscape, but a profuse supply of cut flowers for classic fall arrangements.

November

Arrangements in the house

- Start to pot up bulbs for forcing. Store them over the winter in a dark, cold spot, either sunk into the ground outdoors or in a cold cellar or garage (pages 19–24).
- Continue planting flowering shrubs and ornamental trees.
- Plant shrubs with colorful bark and berries for use in winter arrangements. If you didn't plant red-twig dogwood, holly, and fire thorn in the spring, you can plant these now.
- Plant early-blooming bulbs, such as *Iris reticulata*, *I. danfordiae*, Dutch crocus, and snowdrops for cutting in late January or early February, and some tulips, Dutch crocus, puschkinia, hyacinths, and miniature daffodils for March and April cutting (pages 60–61).
- Plant standard daffodils and May-flowering tulips for cutting in late April and May.

- Dried everlastings, sown in May, can be used for Thanksgiving arrangements.
- Continue using asters and chrysanthemums for arrangements.
- Fire thorn berries are available now for use in autumn arrangements.

What to do in the garden

- Continue to pot up bulbs for forcing.
- Continue planting flowering shrubs, ornamental trees, and shrubs with colorful bark and berries.
- Purchase amaryllis bulbs and start growing them for Christmas displays (pages 75–78).

Holly berries, various grasses, white pine foliage, beautyberry, and pheasant feathers make this Christmas arrangement special. Arrangement by Darlene Cichanowicz.

- Continue planting standard daffodils and May-flowering tulips for cutting in April and May.
- Cut and hang dry the silver foliage of artemisia, dusty miller, and lavender cotton for use in Christmas wreaths and decorations.

- Amaryllis started in November should be just about in bloom for Christmas.
- Use your dried silver foliage in Christmas wreaths and decorations.

December
Arrangements in the house

- Use holly, as well as other berry-producing plants, in Christmas decorations.

What to do in the garden

- Now is the time to select flowering houseplants for bloom in January or February and to finish up any last-minute potting of bulbs for forcing.
- Finally, have a Happy Holiday!

2

Cutting and Conditioning Flowers

· · ·

If you are serious about having beautiful arrangements of flowers in your house throughout the year, you will want them to last more than a day or so. After all, you've invested time and money in growing cut-flower material yourself, as well as in planning arrangements. So, to make your arrangements last as long as possible you must cut, precondition, and condition your material. This chapter will teach you the recommended way to do these things. Special instructions for particular flowers are also included here.

TIME OF DAY TO CUT. The best time to cut flowers and foliage from your garden is early in the morning, while the dew is still on the blossoms. This is because the blossoms have had the long, cool night to revive after the warmth of the previous day.

If, for whatever reason, this is impossible, the second best time to cut is in the late evening, at sunset.

The worst time of the day to cut is from midmorning through evening, that is, during the heat of the day. This is because the rays of the sun and ensuing heat cause the moisture in the blossoms and foliage to evaporate into the air, leaving them in a somewhat stressed condition.

WHAT YOU NEED FOR CUTTING. Bring some sharp clippers or pruning shears to cut woody stalks and a pair of sharp scissors or a sharp knife to cut flower stems. This will ensure clean cuts which do not bruise or tear the delicate stems, thus making it difficult for the stem to absorb water later on.

Also bring a large pail full of air temperature water with you. This will allow you to immerse material immediately after cutting.

HOW TO CUT MATERIAL. Never pull or break flower stems by hand. Always cut with a sharp knife or pruning shears at a *45-degree angle.* You do this in order to expose a larger area of the cut stem to water, thus facilitating greater absorption than if you cut at a 90-degree angle. If possible, always cut the stem below a node. You do this because cutting midpoint between nodes can weaken the plant, affecting the availability and quality of future cutting material.

Select blossoms that are at the proper stage of their blooming cycle. With a few exceptions, almost all blossoms should be cut when buds are tight. If you pick a blossom when it is too tight, it will not develop properly, and if you pick when it has already opened, it will not last long in your arrangement. For example, there is no point in cutting a full-blown rose for an arrangement because the petals will begin to fall even before it reaches a vase. Budding branches of flowering shrubs or trees should be picked when buds are tight so that they can open in the warmth of the house.

Preconditioning Cut Material

There are as many different ways to do this as there are people who arrange flowers. Some say the cut material should be immersed in cold water, some in hot water, some in warm water. I have even come upon one recommendation offered by a professor of horticulture specifying the exact water temperature (110°F). Some say material should be immersed up to the flower bud, others say three quarters of the stems should be immersed. Needless to say, this is all unnecessarily confusing.

As a general rule, when you first bring cut material into the house for preconditioning, room temperature water covering about three quarters of the stem will serve to refresh almost all material.

Remember that the important thing is to get the cut material into water as soon as possible, so be sure to have a pailful of water prepared ahead of time. If you are cutting a large amount of material, have several pails ready, for you do not want to overcrowd the material, possibly damaging some of it.

The reason you immerse the material in water is that it has been separated from its food- and water-seeking roots, so you must try to simulate the work of the roots. The stem of a flower contains tubes called fibrovascular bundles, which transport nourishment from the roots up the stem to the flower. When a stem is cut and left out of water, nature starts to heal the cut by sealing it and closing off the tubes. Without water, the stem relaxes and the flower will wilt. What you want to do is to prevent this healing process and allow the stem to continue to function.

Once you have placed all material in buckets of water it is time to prepare each individual cutting of each plant you have cut. Different types of material require different initial preparation.

Most Cutting Material

This includes most annuals and perennials and many bulb cuttings.

1. One by one, take each cutting from the pail and place the stem in a container filled with six inches of room-temperature water.

2. While the bottom of the stem of the cutting is underwater, using a very sharp knife or scissors, cut one or two inches off the bottom of the cutting at a 45-degree angle. This ensures that

needed water, and not air, will be absorbed into the stem immediately. If you do not use a sharp instrument, the tubes of the flower may be squeezed together when you cut and thus will not absorb water. If the cut is made at a 90-degree angle, that is straight across, the bottom of the stem may ultimately rest on the bottom of the container, thus blocking access to water and clogging it with sediment.

3. While the cutting is underwater, scrape the bottom two inches of each stem with a sharp knife, removing some of the green fiber. This will facilitate water absorption.

4. When you recut the stems of the material underwater, also remove all leaves which will ultimately lie below the waterline in the container that you plan on using for the arrangement. You do this for two reasons. First, if lower leaves are left on the material, water absorbed up through the stem will escape through the leaves and never reach the blossom, causing the blossoms to wilt and die. Secondly, leaves which will be underwater will rot, creating bacteria that will foul the water and clog the tubes of the stems of the cutting material. And third, if you are using a clear glass container for your arrangement, the leaves below the waterline will look messy and detract from the beauty of your creation.

5. Reimmerse the cutting in a pailful of room-temperature water.

6. Mist the flower heads with cool water.

Material with Hard Woody Stems

This includes most flowering shrub and tree material, such as lilacs, dogwoods, azaleas, and camellias, as well as chrysanthemums.

1. Follow steps 1 through 4 described above.

2. Remove the cutting from the water and smash the bottom of it with a hammer.

3. Using a sharp knife, cut a slit two to eight inches long up the bottom of the stem, the length depending on how long the stems are. The cut should be no more than one third the length of the stem. This and step 2 will facilitate water absorption.

4. Reimmerse the cutting in room-temperature water.

5. Mist flower heads with cool water.

Material with Hollow Stems

This includes daffodils, zinnias, Shasta daisies, lupines, dahlias, heliotrope, Transvaal daisies, and poppies.

1. Follow steps 1 and 2 as described on page 10.

2. When you cut flowers with hollow stems, you will notice a sticky white substance oozing from the cut. This is a nutrient and unless contained in the flower stem, the flower will die. And, beyond that, the sap that bleeds from the stems will leak into the water and clog the tubes of these flowers, eventually causing them to die. In order to preserve the flower and prevent the

leaking of sap you must sear the bottom of the cutting. So, remove the cutting from the water, recut the bottom of the stem, and sear the end of it with the flame of a match or candle.

3. Remove any leaves that will fall below the waterline.

4. Reimmerse the cutting in room-temperature water.

5. Mist flower heads with cool water.

Material with Spikes of Florets

This includes snapdragons, delphiniums, and gladiolus.

1. Follow steps 1 through 4 as described on pages 10–11.

2. Remove the small top buds on the flower spikes, as these will never mature and open.

3. Reimmerse the cutting in a pailful of room-temperature water.

4. Mist flower heads with cool water.

Tulips

Harvest tulips at any point from the bud stage to when the flower is half open. Leave as much foliage on the remaining plant as possible so the bulb can mature.

1. Because tulips always wilt almost immediately after cutting, special conditioning must be executed before the usual preconditioning. After picking, wrap the bunch of cuttings with a chimney of stiff nonabsorbent paper, then place this in a pailful of room-temperature water for several hours. This will prevent them from flopping over when you condition them.

2. Then, one by one, take each cutting from the pail and place the stem in a container filled with six inches of room-temperature water.

3. While the bottom of the stem of the cutting is underwater, using a very sharp knife or scissors, at a 45-degree angle, cut to the green part of stem, removing all of the white part, as tulips cannot absorb water through the white part of the stem.

4. When you recut the stems of the material underwater, also remove all leaves which will ultimately lie below the waterline.

5. Rewrap the tulips in the chimney of paper and reimmerse the bunch in a pailful of room-temperature water.

6. Mist the flower heads with cool water.

Roses

Cut roses just as the second petal unfurls. Make sure to cut the stem just above a five- or seven-leaflet leaf rather than a three-leaflet leaf or the stem may cease to bloom.

1. Follow steps 1 through 4 on pages 10–11. If the roses are long-stemmed beauties from a florist, before proceeding, wrap the entire bunch firmly in several layers of wet newspaper. This will ensure that the blossom heads do not droop before conditioning.

2. Cut a slit in the hard wood stem about one inch from the bottom. Then, bruise the bottom inch with a wooden mallet. This will facilitate water absorption.

3. To make cuttings easier to handle, gently remove the thorns. Break each thorn individually, sliding a sharp knife against the base of the spike. Do not slice down from above or you will tear the green bark of the stem. Each thorn should be removed with as clean and isolated a cut as possible, otherwise too much scar tissue will build up around a large wound, again clogging the conducting tubes.

4. Reimmerse the cutting in a pailful of room-temperature water up to the neck of the blossom.

5. Mist flower heads with cool water.

Double checking preconditioning. Once you have preconditioned the cut-flower material, put the pailful of cuttings aside for an hour or so. If the blossoms have wilted somewhat, or do not begin to open up, repeat the process, cutting an additional one or two inches from the stems.

CONDITIONING CUTTING MATERIAL FOR ARRANGEMENTS. Now that you have preconditioned the cutting material, it is time to condition it. Again, there are hundreds of theories about how to go about this. As a general rule, the way to condition flowers for arranging is to immerse them up to their necks in a pailful of *cool* water, in a *cool* place, out of the sun, overnight. Mist flower heads with *cool* water. By the following morning, they should be turgid and ready for arranging.

PROVIDING FOOD FOR CUT FLOWERS. Since the material you have gathered no longer has a food source, that is, a root system, to prolong the life of the cutting, you must provide food. You do this during the overnight conditioning as well as when you are ready to create a permanent arrangement. Helga Dawn, of Southampton, New York, who has been awarded many blue ribbons for her lovely rose arrangements in flower show competition, recommends the chemical flower preservative Floralife, available at garden centers, nurseries, and flo-

rist shops. You simply add this to the water when you condition the cuttings and to the water in the arrangement container according to the manufacturer's instructions.

An alternative is to add one or two drops of chlorine bleach per quart of water, and sugar, at the rate of one teaspoon per quart, to the water. Do this once, before fashioning an arrangement. The chlorine kills bacteria and helps keep the tubes open and the sugar provides glucose, the food which blossoms need to continue to develop in size and color.

Beyond this, a small piece of charcoal placed in the water of an arrangement will help to keep the water pure.

In any case, be sure you allow several hours for the flowers to absorb the food before arranging them.

REVIVING WILTED FLOWERS. If flowers are severely wilted, you can sometimes revive them by recutting the stems underwater and then plunging the flowers up to their necks in warm water for three hours. Then proceed with the particular preconditioning instructions.

KEEPING FLOWERS FRESH. Once you have created your arrangements, do not just put the container somewhere and forget about it. Cut flowers, like any living plant, absorb water and water evaporates. Replenish water daily and the arrangement will last longer. To further prolong the life of the flowers, after several days recut the stems and rearrange the flowers. Be sure to do this underwater as described earlier.

To keep arrangements fresh and to prolong the life of flowers, do not place containers near radiators, fireplaces, heating registers, or in direct sunlight. They will last longer if situated in a cool, but not drafty, location. If need be, during the night, place the arrangement in a cool room.

Special Instructions

Some plants require special attention and should be cut at certain times during the bloom cycle.

Amaryllis *(Hippeastrum)*. Because it has a hollow stem, after cutting, turn the stem upside down and fill it with water. Then, to contain the water, place your thumb over the bottom and plunge into the conditioning container. Condition overnight as described on page 13 in nutrient-fortified water.

Astilbe. Pick when fully open. Split stem ends.

Azaleas and rhododendrons. Cut evergreen and deciduous azaleas and rhododendrons from bud stage to when half of the blossoms on the flower head are open. Be sure to scrape and crush the stems.

Baby's breath *(Gyypsophila)*. Cut sprays of both annual and perennial varieties when they are nearly half open. Immerse the stems and flowers in cold water overnight.

Bellflower *(Campanula)*. Split the stems of woody varieties and sear or plunge ends into boiling water for one minute.

Blanketflower *(Gaillardia)*. Cut when the centers are still tight. Split the stems.

Bleeding heart *(Dicentra)*. Cut when four or five florets show most of their color. Scrape the bottom two inches of the stem.

Camellia. Immerse the entire cutting, flower head and all, in water. Be sure to smash the woody stems with a hammer and remove the bark.

Carnation *(Dianthus)*. If garden-grown, cut when the flowers are half to fully open. When harvesting, cut at a 45-degree angle between the joints or nodes. Recut the stems at a 45-degree angle underwater. Treat florist carnations the same way. After preconditioning and conditioning, place in cold water for one hour or so before arranging in tepid water. Can be dried in a microwave.

Chrysanthemum. Cut when the flowers are fully open. Mums last a long time in arrangements so, after one week, recut and recondition overnight in warm water. You may find that the flowers are still fresh-looking two weeks later. If so, recut again and recondition overnight in warm water.

Clematis. Sear the stem ends over a flame or plunge into boiling water for thirty seconds.

Cockscomb *(Celosia plumosa/cristata)*. Cut when the flowers are three quarters to fully open. Scrape and sear the stem ends over a flame or plunge into very hot water for thirty seconds. Be sure to smash the woody stems with a hammer and remove bark.

Cornflower or bachelor's button *(Centaurea)*. Cut when the flowers are three quarters to fully open. Scrape stems and split in warm water. Precondition and condition overnight in warm water.

Cosmos. Pick the flowers before pollen appears, or force when the buds begin to enlarge. Split the stems.

Crocus, Dutch. Plunge the stems into boiling water for thirty seconds before conditioning in cold water overnight.

Daffodil *(Narcissus)*. Cut when color shows in the bud, and remove foliage sparingly. Precondition and condition as described on pages 11 and 13. Do not recut the stems, or the bleeding will start again. If you do, resear with a match. Be sure to add floral preservative or sugar to the water to extend vase life.

Dahlia. Cut when the flowers are fully open. Since dahlias bleed, the stem ends must be seared with a match for thirty seconds. After searing, prick a hole on the stem with a pin just beneath the flower head to prevent airlock. Precondition and condition them overnight in warm rather than cool water.

Daisy, Michaelmas *(Aster)*. Cut when the flowers have just opened. Remove all leaves below water level. Scrape, split, and boil stem ends for thirty seconds. Add sugar to the water at the rate of one teaspoon per quart. Recutting underwater every few days extends life.

Daisy, Transvaal *(Gerbera).* Cut when the flowers are three quarters to fully open, that is when two rows of pollen are fully open. Scrape the stems or sear stem ends in a flame or plunge the stems into very hot water for thirty seconds. Be sure to smash the woody stems with a hammer to facilitate water intake. Precondition and condition as for dahlias.

Daisy, Shasta *(Chrysanthemum maximum).* Cut when half to fully open. Remove all foliage below water level. Sear stems with a match for thirty seconds.

Delphinium. Cut when half of the flower spike shows color. Snap off the top buds. Because it has a hollow stem, after cutting, turn the stem upside down and fill it with water. Then, place your thumb over the bottom to hold the water in the stem and immerse in cool conditioning water overnight. To extend vase life, be sure to add a floral preservative or sugar to the arrangement water, at the rate of one teaspoon per quart.

Dogwood *(Cornus).* Cut when the flowers are three quarters open, that is when the bracts have opened but before the pollen appears. Scrape the stems and sear the stem ends in a flame or plunge the stems into very hot water for thirty seconds. Be sure to smash the woody stems with a hammer and remove the bark.

Everlastings. For both fresh and dried use, cut when all of the flowers have opened.

Ferns. Submerge in cold water until fronds are turgid, two to four hours for varieties with coarse foliage and four to eight hours for varieties with delicate foliage.

Foliage plants. Condition in warm water overnight.

Forget-me-not, annual *(Myosotis).* Cut when the flowers are half open.

Forsythia. Cut branches just as they start to flower.

Foxglove *(Digitalis).* Cut flowers when one fourth to one half of the florets are open and place im-mediately in warm water. Because it has a hollow stem, after cutting turn the stem upside down and fill it with water. Then place your thumb over the bottom to hold the water in the stem and immerse in cool conditioning water overnight. To extend vase life, be sure to add a floral preservative or sugar to the arrangement water, at the rate of one teaspoon per quart.

Gladiolus. Cut as the second floret opens. Scrape stems. Snap off the top buds.

Globe thistle *(Echinops).* Cut when the flowers are three quarters to fully open. Scrape the stems or sear the stem ends in a flame or plunge the stems into very hot water for thirty seconds. Be sure to smash the woody stems with a hammer to facilitate water intake.

Grape hyacinth *(Muscari).* Split the stems and condition in cold water overnight.

Heliotrope *(Heliotropus).* Cut when the flowers are three quarters to fully open. Sear the stems in a flame.

Hellebore *(Helleborus).* Singe or place the stem ends in boiling water for thirty seconds.

Hosta. Cut when three or four flowers have opened. Split stems and condition in cold water nearly up to blossoms.

Hyacinth, Dutch *(Hyacinthus orientalis).* It can-not absorb water through the white part of the stem. Cut to the green.

Iris, Bearded or German. Cut when first bud is nearly open. Add one teaspoon sugar per quart of arrangement water.

Iris, Siberian *(Iris sibirica).* Cut as the first bud opens. Do not cut off the foliage.

Larkspur *(Consolida ambigua).* Cut when the flowers are one third open. Snap off the top buds. Be sure to add floral preservative or sugar to the water to extend vase life.

Lavender *(Lavandula).* Cut when half of the flow-ers on the spike are open. Split the stems.

Lilac *(Syringa).* Cut when the flowers are half to

fully open. Scrape and crush the stems with a hammer. Remove the bark and place the pounded stem in denatured alcohol for *only* three to five minutes. Then precondition and condition as for other woody plants (page 11).

Lily *(Lilium).* Cut as the first bud opens. Cut no more than one third of the stem or the bulb will not mature. Remove the stamens with scissors as the pollen will stain fabric and skin.

Lily-of-the-valley *(Convallaria majalis).* Cut when the top buds are still closed or just beginning to show color.

Lupine *(Lupinus).* Cut when half of the flowers on the spike are open. Because it has a hollow stem, after cutting turn the stem upside down and fill it with water. Then, place your thumb over the bottom to hold the water in the stem, and plunge into the conditioning water. Condition overnight in nutrient-fortified water and be sure to add floral preservative or sugar to the water to extend vase life.

Magnolia, saucer *(Magnolia × soulangiana).* Cut when the blossoms are about ready to open. Scrape stems and sear the stem ends in a flame or plunge the stems into very hot water for thirty seconds. Be sure to smash the woody stems with a hammer and remove the bark.

Magnolia, star *(M. stellata).* Cut when the blossoms are about ready to open. Treat as for saucer magnolia.

Marigold *(Tagetes).* Cut when the flowers are fully open. Marigolds lose their offensive smell if one tablespoon of sugar is put in the arrangement water. Recutting underwater every few days extends life.

Marigold, pot *(Calendula).* Cut when the flowers are fully open. Scrape the stems. Condition overnight.

Pansy *(Viola × Wittrockiana).* After cutting, precondition by immersing in water for several hours, flower head and all. Then condition in cool water overnight.

Peony *(Paeonia).* Cut anytime from when the bud has colored to when the flower is fully open. Scrape and split the stem and plunge into deep hot water for four hours. Then precondition and condition in cool water as described on pages 11 and 13.

Phlox. Cut above a stem joint when half the flowers are open. Condition overnight in cold water.

Poppy, oriental *(Papaver orientale).* Cut poppies the night before the bloom opens. Sear the stem ends immediately after cutting. Be sure to add floral preservative or sugar to water to extend vase life.

Snapdragon *(Antirrhinum).* Cut when the flowers are half to fully open. Scrape the stems; snap off the top buds. Precondition and condition overnight in tepid rather than cool water.

Striped squill *(Puschkinia).* Plunge the stems into boiling water for thirty seconds before conditioning in cold water overnight.

Sweet William *(Dianthus barbatus).* Cut at a slant above joints. Split larger stems.

Violet *(Viola).* Cut when the flowers are half to fully open. Soak in cold water, blossom and all, for a half hour, then wrap in a damp paper towel and refrigerate for two to three hours.

Wisteria. Cut when the first flowers of the cluster are open. Split stems. Spray flowers every few days to keep them from drying out.

Yarrow *(Achillea).* Pick when half the flowers are open. Foliage often wilts.

Zinnia. Cut when the flowers are almost fully open. Remove almost all the leaves. Sear the stems with a match for thirty seconds.

3

Forcing

. . .

Forcing Branches of Flowering Shrubs

While you're nurturing your Christmas gift plants and filling your house with arrangements of dried flowers and evergreens, late January is also the time to start gathering branches of flowering shrubs and trees from your garden for early forcing. Doing this will insure you plenty of cut-flower material to brighten the house during the bleak days of February and March.

There are many species appropriate for cutting and forcing. (See the chart on page 20.) Note that these shrubs and trees all bloom in the spring and that as winter wanes, less and less forcing time is necessary to bring dormant branches to bloom.

When you force flowering shrub and tree branches, you are essentially playing games with mother nature by providing the warmth, moisture, and light conditions of the plant's natural growth period well before its time. Flower buds have already formed on the shrubs and trees in your garden by the time winter arrives. If you look carefully, you can see them, well protected by layers and layers of bud scales.

By late January, the cold-weather dormancy requirements of some species have been satisfied and branches can be cut for forcing. Other species need till February or March for their dormancy requirements to be met.

Early spring-blooming shrubs sport blossoms which look stunning in an arrangement.
Here andromeda, camellias, flowering quince, and spirea combine beautifully.
Arrangement by Lucille Siracusano, Feather Hill Country Flowers and Gifts.

We used to speak of a January thaw, that is, those balmy days in January following frigid December temperatures. However, of late, particularly in the East, there have been no Arctic temperatures in December and few in January or February. At any rate, on a balmy late January day, quite common these days, go out into the garden around high noon to cut. This is the time of the day when the buds are filled with the most sap. Bring a sharp knife or sharp pruning shears with you and cut your forcing material. When you cut, look for younger branches which contain large buds. These usually will provide the most profuse display.

As you cut, remember that pruning is healthy for the plant and that this is the time of year to do it. Select branches with interesting curves that are 1½ to 3 feet long. When you cut, be sure to follow basic pruning practices. That is, cut to the mother branch, leaving little if any stub. Also keep in mind that you do not want to destroy the natural spectacular spring-blooming beauty of the shrub or tree, so when you take your cuttings, try to maintain the natural shape of the plant.

Once you have collected your cuttings, it is time to condition them. What you do when you force bloom is try to emulate nature, allowing the blossoms to develop slowly and thus forcing natural-size flowers with vibrant color.

After you've taken your cuttings, bring them indoors and smash the bottom of the stems with a hammer. Although a clean cut at an angle with a knife or pruning shears will usually allow water to be absorbed by the cutting, mashing the stem is easy and foolproof, assuring the absorption of water.

The Cut-flower Garden

There are many ways to provide the water necessary for the cuttings. Some people recommend wrapping the branches in wet burlap or newspaper for several days before immersing them in water. Others suggest putting the branches in the bathtub and spraying them with water several times a day for several days before immersing them. However, after trying both these methods, I found that the easiest and most foolproof method was to place the cuttings in a large pail of water and add either floral preservative, available at garden centers and nurseries, or a tablespoon of sugar and a few drops of bleach. These additives assure a long life for the branches by lessening the likelihood of bacterial attack and keeping the absorption tubes in the stems unclogged. Then place the pail in a cool, dark spot. Every few days, change the water, being sure to add floral preservative or sugar and bleach each time you do. After several weeks, the buds will begin to swell. Once swollen, move the pail to a cool, well-lighted area, out of direct sunlight. The light will force bloom and flower color development.

Another way to force bloom is to fill a pail three-quarters full with water. Set the pail in a large, clear plastic dress bag, the kind that comes from the cleaners. Place the branches in the water and add a cotton ball that has been soaked in sudsy ammonia. Tie the bag closed and place in a warm, well-lighted place, but out of direct sunlight. The gas emitted from the ammonia-soaked ball, which is contained in the plastic bag, will help to force bloom.

Once color appears in the buds, it is time to use the cuttings in arrangements. Tall vases are particularly appropriate for displaying these graceful branches. Do not wait until the blossoms have opened to do this, for you will miss the pleasure of watching them unfurl. When you display your arrangement, place it in a cool area (65°F or lower), out of direct sunlight. This will allow the buds to develop and open slowly, resulting in finer quality blossoms. If the temperature is higher, the development of the flowers will accelerate, quality will diminish, and display life will be shortened.

Planting instructions for species mentioned in the chart appear in the shrub and flowering tree individual entries in chapter 10.

Forcing Bulbs

Each year, in late winter or early spring, you've probably noticed pots of blooming tulips, daffodils, and other bulbs on display at garden centers,

If you force several containers of bright yellow mini-daffodils and deep purple Iris reticulata *and* muscari, *you'll have a wealth of colorful flower material to brighten your house during the winter months.*

Flowering Shrubs and Trees for Forced Bloom

SPECIES	FORCING TIME	VASE LIFE
Cut in January		
Azalea*/***	3–6 weeks, depending on species	5–10 days
Rhododendron Gable hybrids (Gable hybrid Azalea)***	6 weeks	5–10 days
R. molle × *R. occidentale* × *R. arborescens* (Knab Hill and Exbury azalea)*	3 weeks	5–10 days
R. mucronulatum (Korean rhododendron)*	3 weeks	1 week
R. obtusum hybrids (Kurume azalea hybrids)***	6 weeks	5–10 days
Forsythia intermedia	3 weeks	1 week
Hamamelis spp. (Witch hazel)*	1 week	3–5 days
Prunus persica (Flowering peach)**	4–5 weeks	1 week
P. × *sieboldii* (Flowering cherry)**	3–4 weeks	1–2 weeks
P. × *blireiana* (Flowering plum)**	3–4 weeks	10 days
Cut in February		
Azalea*/***	3–6 weeks, depending on species	5–10 days
Chaenomeles japonica (Japanese scarlet quince)*	3–5 weeks	4–7 days
Forsythia × *intermedia*	2 weeks	1 week
Magnolia × *soulangiana* (Saucer magnolia)**	2 weeks	1 week
Prunis sieboldii (Flowering cherry)**	3 weeks	1–2 weeks
Rhododendron mucronulatum (Korean rhododendron)*	2 weeks	1 week
Salix discolor (French pink pussy willow)*	1 week	2–3 weeks
Cut in March		
Cornus florida (Flowering dogwood)**	2–4 weeks	7–10 days
Chaenomeles japonica (Japanese scarlet quince)*	2 weeks	4–7 days
Deutzia gracilis rosea	2–3 weeks	2 weeks
Forsythia intermedia	1 week	1 week
Malus spp. (Flowering crab apple)**	2–3 weeks	1 week
Prunus sieboldii (Flowering cherry)**	2–3 weeks	1–2 weeks
Spiraea prunifolia (Bridal wreath)*	2–3 weeks	7–10 days
Syringa spp. (Lilac)*	4–6 weeks	1 week

*   Flowering deciduous shrub

**   Flowering tree

*** Flowering broad-leaved shrub

nurseries, and in florist shops. If you've ever wondered how bulbs are "forced," it is quite easy. You can do it at home by following these instructions. And just think of the joy of having your house filled with cheerful blooming spring bulbs in February and March.

SELECTING CONTAINERS. Although you can grow bulbs in just about any kind of container imaginable, the traditional "bulb pan" in clay or plastic is probably the best, for essential drainage holes are provided. As a rule, the pot should be about twice as deep as the length of the bulbs. In other words, a bulb which measures two inches from top to bottom should be potted in a four-inch-deep pot.

SOIL MIXTURE. A good soil mixture to use is Reddi-Mix or Terra-lite, available in garden centers or nurseries. Or you can use any soil mix recommended for starting seedlings. If you wish to make your own soil mix, combine one part packaged potting soil, one part sphagnum peat moss, and one part horticultural or builder's sand. Add one cup perlite or horticultural vermiculite to each quart of soil mix. Be sure to wet the sphagnum peat moss thoroughly and squeeze until almost dry before adding it to your homemade mix.

PLANTING. First, cover the drainage holes with pebbles, rocks, broken flowerpot shards, or the white plastic "popcorn" used by mail-order houses to ship merchandise. Then fill the pot about two-thirds full with soil mix. Check the depth by placing a bulb on the soil surface so that the tip of the bulb is a half inch below the rim of the pot. Adjust the soil level if necessary. Set more bulbs on the soil, as many as the pot will accommodate, as long as they do not touch each other. Continue to fill the pot with soil mix. Do not firm the soil; bulb roots require loosely packed soil to grow properly.

If you are planting tulip bulbs, it pays to take special care in placing the bulbs in the pot. The first leaves tulip bulbs produce grow from the flat side of the bulb, so place the bulbs with their flat sides facing the outside of the pot. The ultimate effect will be more aesthetically pleasing, with the large leaves serving as an outer display of foliage.

Once planted, the pots should be watered thoroughly. Fill in any cavities with more soil mix if necessary. Be sure to label each pot, so when it comes time to force bloom, you will know which is which.

THE CHILLING PROCESS. In order to bring bulbs to bloom before their normal time, you must provide a cold environment. In nature, they require below-freezing temperatures in order to bloom. There are three different ways to replicate this.

1. You can sink pots into a cold frame outdoors, covering them with a six- to eight-inch layer of salt hay or sand. However, this entails making trips out into the garden in the dead of winter to check on their progress. Often, in very cold weather, it is difficult to remove the protective covering because it is frozen stiff. But, if you have no other option, this is the way to do it.

2. Much easier and equally as effective is to place the pots in the cellar or in an unheated garage. The temperature ideally should stay between 30° and 50°F. Cover the pots with black plastic so that no light will fall on the bulbs, or use several thicknesss of newspaper. In general, the pots will need to be watered approximately every four weeks. Even so, it is a good idea to check the soil every week; if it is dry to the touch, water moderately. Good root growth is essential for successful forcing; when in doubt, favor the longer period recommended in the accompanying chart.

3. The third method is to chill the bulbs in the refrigerator. Simply place potted bulbs inside and check every now and then to see if watering is necessary. Do NOT place pots in the freezer.

FORCING BLOOM. After the prescribed cooling period, when shoots have emerged and are about two to three inches high, it is time to move the pots to a warmer position to begin the forcing process. At this point the shoots will be a light yellow-green color. Although each bulb is handled slightly differently, the general procedure is to set the pots in a cool (55° to 60°F) location, either in darkness or bright, indirect light, for a period of three to five weeks.

During this period bulbs will develop strong top growth. Check the soil occasionally and water if necessary. (NOTE: To ensure tall stems in hyacinths rather than short stubby ones, fashion a cylinder about eight inches tall by one and a half inches in diameter out of heavy paper and place it over the emerging hyacinth flower stem. The semidark condition will cause the stem to elongate, thus looking more natural. When the stem is about six inches high, remove the cylinder.)

As soon as flower buds appear, place the pots in a cool location (50° to 65°F) that receives direct sunlight. Once the buds begin to show color, they can be moved wherever they will be admired. Keep in mind, though, the cooler the temperatures, especially at night, the longer the bulbs will stay in bloom. Under optimum conditions—no warmer than 65°F and indirect light—plants should stay in bloom for a week to ten days.

POSTBLOOM CARE. Although tulips almost never bloom again once they have been forced and should be discarded, other types of bulbs will bloom in your garden a year or two after forcing. However, they cannot be forced again the following year. If you wish to plant your forced bulbs for outdoor enjoyment, you must care for the plants. After the flowers begin to fade, feed once with a liquid plant fertilizer at the recommended strength. When the flowers are spent, cut the stems off at the soil line. Do NOT cut the foliage. Continue watering moderately until the foliage withers and turns brown.

When it is completely withered, remove the bulbs from the pot, cut off all foliage and roots, and remove the soil. Then place the bulbs in labeled paper bags. Make a few holes in the bag for ventilation and store in a dark, dry place until fall, when you can plant them in the ground.

TIMING If you want to have bulbs in bloom by a particular date, pay special attention to the last line of the following entries. If, for example, you want to have hyacinths in bloom for New Year's Day, count back eight to thirteen weeks to arrive at a planting date—sometime in the first two weeks of October would be safe. The cold rooting period offers some leeway, but never force bulbs that haven't been in the cold for the minimum number of weeks specified for each kind of bulb. You can, however, leave them in longer than the maximum number of weeks recommended, if necessary. If you order bulbs that have been prechilled you can subtract approximately two weeks from the cold rooting period and one week from the time needed for forcing.

Crocus, Dutch

Rooting: 6 to 10 weeks in a dark location at 30° to 50°F, until shoots are 1½ inches tall.
Forcing: Bright, indirect light, 50° to 55°F for approximately 1 week. Move to full sun but still cool location until buds show color.
Flowering: Move to indirect light, cool temperatures (55° to 60°F) for longest flowering.
Total weeks to flowering: 9 to 13.

Hyacinth, Dutch
(Hyacinthus orientalis)

Rooting: 6 to 10 weeks at 30° to 50°F in a dark location.

Forcing: 10 days to 2 weeks at 50° to 55°F in a dark location. Move into bright, indirect light when shoots are 4 to 5 inches tall. Buds should show color in 7 to 10 days. See note on page 22 about fashioning cylinders for elongating hyacinth stems.

Flowering: Keep in bright, indirect light at 60° to 65°F for longest flowering.

Total weeks to flowering: 8 to 13.

Hyacinth, Grape
(Muscari armeniacum)

Rooting: 6 to 10 weeks in a dark location at 30° to 50°F, until shoots are 1½ inches tall.

Forcing: Bright, indirect light and temperatures of 50° to 55°F for approximately 1 week. Move to full sun, but still cool location until buds show color.

Flowering: Move to indirect light with cool temperatures (55° to 60°F) for longest flowering.

Total weeks to flowering: 10 to 14.

Iris danfordiae and I. reticulata

Rooting: 6 to 8 weeks in a dark location at 30° to 50°F, until shoots are 1½ inches tall.

Forcing: Bright, indirect light and temperatures of 50° to 55°F for approximately 1 week. Move to full sun, but still cool location until buds show color.

Flowering: Move to indirect light with cool temperatures (55° to 60°F) for longest flowering.

Total weeks to flowering: 8 to 12.

Lily-of-the-Valley
(Convallaria majalis)

In order to force lilies-of-the-valley, you must purchase pretreated bulbs from mail-order houses. Because the treatment the bulbs receives is complicated, you cannot readily do this yourself. Occasionally, local nurseries or garden centers also offer them. They are preplanted in containers. Simply follow the instructions included.

Narcissus, Including Daffodils

(This information does not apply to *Narcissus tazetta*—paperwhites. See below.)

Rooting: 10 to 12 weeks in a dark location at 30° to 50°F. Shoots should be 3 to 4 inches tall before moving into light.

Forcing: Bright, indirect light, 60° to 65°F for 3 or 4 days, then full sun until blossoms open, approximately 3 to 5 weeks.

Flowering: Move back into bright, indirect light at 55° to 70°F to prolong life of the flowers.

Total weeks to flowering. 13 to 17.

Paperwhites
(Narcissus tazetta)

Paperwhite narcissus are among the easiest bulbs to force. They are available all over the country in garden centers and nurseries in late fall and on into the winter. They are virtually foolproof and provide flowering plants for almost any kind of indoor environment. Some mail-order houses offer preplanted narcissus in bulb pans; all you have to do is provide them certain basic growing conditions. Once paperwhites have bloomed, they will not bloom again, either indoors or planted in the garden, so dispose of them and purchase new ones the following year.

When the bulbs arrive by mail, or after you've purchased them, store in a cool, dark place until ready to plant. The refrigerator is good: do not, however, store them in the freezer.

Rooting: When ready to plant, select a shallow bulb pan or container *without drainage holes*. Tender narcissus grow well in pebbles, small stones, or broken flowerpot shards. Rinse all the materials thoroughly until the draining water is clear. Place about an inch of planting material in the bottom of the bulb pan. Set the bulbs 1½ to 2 inches apart so that two thirds of the bulb is covered with the material. Fill the bulb container about half full with water, allow it to settle for about thirty minutes, then pour off any excess by gently tipping the container. Place in a cool (50° to 60°F) location with little or no light and no risk of frost for about 2 weeks. Test root development by gently turning the bulbs. Every day check the moistness of the planting medium. If it feels dry to the touch, add a little water.

Forcing: When the bulbs are firmly rooted, move the pots to a location receiving strong light but no direct sunlight, where temperature is cool (between 55° and 60°F). Occasionally, the vig-

orous roots will actually heave the bulbs out of the planting medium. If this happens, gently work them down and add more planting material if necessary. Do not force them down or you will injure the tender roots.

Flowering: Once they are in bloom, they can be moved to any location, including one getting little light.

Total weeks to flowering: 3 to 5, depending on the variety and time of year. Those started from October to December take 4 to 5 weeks to flower. Those started from January to March take 3 to 4 weeks to flower; however, the stems will be shorter.

Tulips

Rooting: 12 to 14 weeks at approximately 30° to 50°F in a dark location.

Forcing: Approximately 10 days to 2 weeks in a cool (55° to 60°F) location in bright, indirect light. Move to full sun, same temperature, for 2 weeks, or until buds show color.

Flowering: Bright indirect light at 60° to 65°F for longest flowering.

Total weeks to flowering: 14 to 16.

4

Drying Flowers

. . .

There are a number of traditional ways to dry material for fall and winter flower arrangements. Some are centuries old, others more recent, and the latest, inspired by space-age technology, brand spanking new. Some are more effective than others, however. I have tried them all and have come up with some of my own conclusions. Let's start with the traditional ways of drying material first.

Hang Drying

Certainly the oldest method known, hang drying remains the most effective. Here's how you do it.

1. Collect herbs or flowers from the cut-flower garden. *Be sure you pick them with long stems.* Refer to the individual entries to determine which particular plants are suitable for this drying method.

2. Before hanging up to dry, *strip all the leaves from the stems of flowers* you wish to dry.

3. With six stems or stalks to a bunch, either tie the bunch together with twine or wrap a rubber band from the end. Rubber bands are more effective for binding, since, as the stems shrink, the

Artist Jaqueline Penney creates dried arrangements and then includes them in her paintings.

rubber bands will continue to hold them tight.

4. Hang the bunches *upside down* in a dry, warm, dark place for two days to two weeks, depending on the particular plant you are drying, since some dry more quickly than others. If you don't have a dark location, select a place that is out of strong sun, as light tends to fade the colors of drying material. If you do not have the option of a dim or dark place or a place out of strong

sunlight, cover each bunch of material with a paper bag, tying the bag closed with string, then hanging bag and all in the drying area.

There are many places in the home that are suitable for hanging material for drying—closets, attics, dry cellars, garages, outdoor sheds. However, you might want to think in terms of using the drying material as part of your interior decor. What could be more attractive than bundles of drying herbs and flowers hanging from the ceiling in the kitchen or dining room, or even the living room for that matter? If you decide to use the kitchen for drying, however, avoid placing material near the stove or sink, as steam and spray can impede drying. Bathrooms are not suitable for drying because of the damp conditions.

There are many ways to hang cut-flower material. You can drive nails or pegs into walls, ceilings, beams, or planks and hang individual varieties of herbs and flowers on them. You can use antique or reproduction herb-drying racks, old laundry racks, swivel towel racks, or blanket stands hung on walls or on the floor. Or you can make your own racks; it's a matter of simple carpentry, of nailing lath on a frame. You can copy a photograph of a rack that appeals to you. Perhaps the easiest, but least picturesque, method is to tie the bunches to a clothes hanger hung on a rod or hook. Just about anything which will support a hanging bunch of drying material is suitable. *But be sure when you hang the material that the bunches are far enough apart so that they don't tangle or crush each other and so that air circulates around and between them.* This is to hasten the drying process.

5. When *bone*-dry—and all material *must* be bone-dry when stored or it will turn into an ugly, mildewed, rotten mess—remove the material from the hanging area. Store different varieties separately. Place in airtight containers (I find plastic shoe boxes perfect for this purpose), and store until ready to use in dried flower arrangements.

The hang-drying process is as easy as that. *But not quite!*

In most parts of the country, spring and fall are very pleasant seasons of the year, mild and not particularly wet. However, along with summer come heat and humidity! During the "dog days" of July and August, after a week or so, material that is hang dried can begin to sport mold and mildew. A good idea is to start the drying process by hanging the material for a few days, then, if it is unduly damp, finishing it off by oven drying. This process is explained on pages 29–30.

When you place dried material in airtight containers, add about two tablespoons of uncooked rice to every container. This will absorb any moisture left in the material or in the container and prevent the advent of mold.

If you notice some deterioration of the collected material, closely examine it for small moths. Tiny unseen moth eggs, which may have been on the material when harvested, can hatch into tiny larvae, nibbling away at the planting material and ultimately turning into pesky small moths. To avoid this, place five or six mothballs in each container and again cover them tightly. Of course, when you are ready to use the material it will smell of camphor. However, once aired, after about a week, all trace of camphor smell will vanish.

Grasses gathered from the wild, along with seedpods and autumn foliage, provide the vertical lines so attractive in this arrangement. Arrangement by Barbara Woodward.

Air Drying

Another traditional method is called air drying. To do this you will need flat surfaces through which air can circulate. Some options are old window screens set up on a supporting platform (you can use bricks or boxes as support), flat baskets, or cotton muslin attached to lath frames or hung up somewhere like a hammock. If space is at a premium, you can devise a system of stacking drying trays one on top of another, so long as air can circulate between them. Drying trays are for sale at many herb or health-food shops, at some garden centers or nurseries, and through mail-order sources (see Sources).

This system can be used to dry yarrow, delphiniums, larkspur, zinnias, carnations, calendulas, and bachelor's buttons. Here's how you do it.

1. You can air dry cut-flower material in closets, attics, dry cellars, garages, outdoor sheds, anywhere that is dry, warm, and out of strong sunlight. Air drying in an outdoor shed or garage is usually *not* recommended, because nighttime damp air can cause mildew and mold to form on the material. As with hang drying, if you decide to use the kitchen for drying, avoid placing material near the stove or sink, as steam and spray can impede drying; bathrooms are not suitable for the same reasons.

2. Cut drying material from the garden after the dew has evaporated from the flower heads.

3. If you are drying flowers with stems, lay them down in a random manner, but don't let them overlap.

4. Each day, turn the cut material around. The material should be dry in two to ten days, depending on the humidity in the air and the moisture in the leaves and flowers. If humid conditions slow down the drying process, and mildew and mold become evident, finish drying in an oven (see opposite). Store the dried material as described on page 27.

Water Drying

This is another of the old-fashioned, traditional ways to dry material. I tried it and found that considerably more time was involved in the drying process. Hang drying and air drying are more effective methods. However, it is an easy method requiring no preparation. It is effective for drying gift bouquets or, since no attention is required, in the event you must be away from home, it might serve your purposes. There are some flowers, hydrangeas, grasses, and bells of Ireland, which dry better with this method than others.

1. Harvest cutting material after the morning dew has evaporated or place the gift bouquet of flowers in a container filled about one quarter full with water.

2. Place the container in a warm area out of the sun. The water will slowly evaporate, and the flowers will dry slowly and naturally. This process takes anywhere from one to two weeks.

3. To be sure the material is bone-dry, finish off drying in the oven (see below). Store as described on page 27.

Oven Drying

Oven drying cut-flower material came along with the advent of modern ovens, when it became possible to control temperature. In the unlikely event that you do not have space to hang or air dry material, or should you need material in short order, you can dry in the oven. And, beyond that, it is a good idea to subject all hang-dried or air-dried material to several hours of oven drying to ensure it is bone dry and to avoid mildew and mold forming. Here's how you do it.

1. Set the oven at 100°F and leave the door slightly ajar, so that any lingering moisture can escape.

2. Set the material on one or more cookie sheets, one layer deep, and place in the oven.

3. Watch carefully and turn the material every fifteen minutes. The drying will take anywhere from fifteen minutes to several hours, depending on the type of plant.

4. When the material is crisp and brittle, remove from the oven. Store as described on page 27.

Microwave Drying

Drying flowers and leaves in a microwave oven is the latest method of preparing cut-flower material, and it is one of the quickest and most effective, for flowers retain their brilliant hues and foliage its rich green color when dried this way.

Flowers best suited for this drying method are pansies, roses, chrysanthemums, tulips, carnations, Dutch iris, dogwood, marigolds, and peonies. The smaller or more delicate flowers usually do not dry well when microwaved; however, there's no reason why you can't experiment, vis-à-vis the old adage, "nothing ventured, nothing gained."

Here's how you do it. (Keep in mind that you must not leave the microwave oven unattended while drying material.)

1. Fill any microwave-safe container with a quantity of silica gel, usually available at craft shops, and in some garden centers and nurseries. Microwave on full power for one minute, until the crystals turn bright blue.

2. Place about one inch of the dried, warm silica gel in a shallow rectangular ovenproof baking dish or plastic container. It is best to dry one flower at a time until you have some experience with this method of drying. Place the flower on the bed of warm crystals and carefully cover it

so that the crystals completely cover the blossom. Be sure the flower isn't crushed or distorted.

3. Dry for one minute at full power. Check the blossom. If it is not thoroughly dry, dry for another minute. Check the blossom again, and if not thoroughly dry, dry for another minute. Then, continue drying at thirty-second increments until the blossom is thoroughly dry. Most flowers take between one and three and a half minutes. Those with fleshier petals take the most time to dry thoroughly.

4. Let the flower remain in the crystals for twenty to thirty minutes before gently pouring them off and removing the flower.

NOTE: If blossoms are consistently so brittle that they shatter when removed from the silica gel, place a dish of water in the oven along with the silica gel container when drying.

Drying in Silica Gel

This is perhaps the best method for drying larger, whole flowers. The old-fashioned, traditional way of doing this is to use salt and/or sand; however, this can be messy, often takes six to eight weeks for drying, and consistent results are never assured. However, if you use silica gel, available in craft shops, florist supply stores, some florist shops, and through mail-order houses, and follow the instructions carefully, success is almost always achieved.

Whole roses, mini-rosebuds, delphiniums, camellias, lilies, daffodils, calendulas, and other large blossoms can be successfully dried in this manner.

One advantage to drying with silica gel is that the blossoms retain considerable color intensity. And, although you might opt for arrangements in subdued colors, a few bright blossoms add a lovely, distinctive touch to your creations.

And beyond preserving the brilliant color of larger flowers, more fragile blossoms, such as those of cosmos, which do not dry well when hang-, air- or oven-dried, dry quite nicely in silica gel.

If you purchase a silica gel flower drying kit, complete instructions for drying blossoms are usually included. However, if you purchase a quantity of silica gel, here's how you use it.

Harvesting the flowers. Gather the blossoms on a sunny day, in late morning or early afternoon when the early morning dew has evaporated. Do not gather after rain or in the evening when the blossoms are wet. Try to select flowers that are at the peak of their bloom, as these will retain their brilliant color and hold together better when dried.

Drying the material

1. Fill any airtight, flat container, such as a metal cookie container or plastic refrigerator container, with about one inch of silica gel.

2. Place the flower heads facing up in the powder. If the blossoms are flat-petaled, like daisies and gerberas, place them facedown in the powder. Press them gently into the silica gel mixture, making sure that the insides of the blossoms are also covered with the powder.

3. Sprinkle powder over the entire blossom and in between the flower petals until the entire flower or leaf is completely covered. As you cover blossoms with the powder, be careful not to disturb the natural arrangement of the petals.

4. If your chosen container is airtight, simply place the lid on top and seal. If not, seal the seam of the box with freezer or masking tape.

5. The most important aspect of drying flowers successfully in silica gel is to be sure the flowers are dry but not too dry, that is, so brittle that they shatter when you remove them from the powder. You will have to experiment with each flower you dry to determine the correct timing. If they aren't dry enough when you remove them from the powder, the flowers will wilt, even if stored in an airtight box. Check the flowers every day. It takes roughly two to three days for thin-petaled flowers to dry, five to seven days for fleshier flower heads.

6. When the flower or leaves are ready, gently remove them from the powder with a slotted spoon.

7. If any powder remains clinging to petals or leaves, gently brush it off with a soft watercolor paintbrush.

8. Store the flowers and leaves in an airtight container until ready to use. Place a small quantity of silica gel in the bottom of the container to absorb any moisture which might remain, and to guard against any dampness. As with the microwave method, there is no insect infestation in silica dried material, so adding mothballs to storage jars is unnecessary.

5

The Basics of Flower Arranging

. . .

Tools and Materials

Although it is possible to create very beautiful arrangements without using special materials, a small investment in a few basic aids opens up a vast new world of design possibilities. The following materials are usually available in craft shops and often in florist shops. You may already have some of these in your cellar, barn, garage, or tossed under the sink.

Wire. Wire is used to strengthen hollow stems in extravagant arrangements as well as to create pliable stems for wreath, garland, and posy arrangements. Fine-gauge wire, often called reel rose wire or reel wire, and stub wire are usually available at craft or florist shops. However, hardware stores carry an infinite variety of wire, and usually the price is cheaper than for "special flower arranging wire." After all, wire is wire, and as long as it is thin and easy to work with, it will do fine.

Dry foam blocks. These are small blocks of Styrofoam material which absorb water. They are soaked in water and then placed on the bottom of low containers. Flower stems are then stuck into the foam, and the bottom of the arrangement is masked with foliage or sphagnum moss. They are indispensable for creating arrangements in shallow containers, and are usually available in craft shops and florist shops.

Florists' spikes and adhesive floral clay. Also available in craft and florist shops, these are used to secure foam blocks in containers. The small spikes adhere to the container with the aid of the adhesive floral

A potpourri of rose varieties, arranged in the round form in this antique covered vegetable dish, can be used as a table centerpiece or placed on an end table to enhance the living-room decor. Arrangement by Helga Dawn.

clay. This special clay, which is waterproof, holds fast even when submerged in water. (Modeling clay and even chewing gum are sometimes used as substitutes, though they cannot secure spikes to a container effectively.) After the spike is secured to the container, the foam block is pressed down onto the spike. These two simple supplies will prevent arrangements from toppling over in low containers.

Knives and shears. Although special florists' scissors are usually available in craft or florist shops, ordinary sharp kitchen knives, pruning shears, wire cutters, and scissors should take care of all the cutting you will have to do.

Chicken wire. Available in hardware stores or home improvement centers, small squares of chicken wire can be stuffed into large containers to help hold flower stems in place in an arrangement.

Funnels. These are special small containers which hold water, and are used to hold several small cut flowers. They can be inserted into the soil around houseplants, or into foam blocks to dress up foliage or foliage arrangements. They are usually available in craft and florist shops.

Florists' tape. Also available in craft and florist shops, this is used to tie the stems in an arrangement together; however, in most cases simple string will accomplish the same end. It is also used

The Basics of Flower Arranging
· · ·33· · ·

to conceal wire which you might use in securing the stems of arrangements. This is only necessary, though, if you are using a clear glass container.

Sphagnum moss. Available in craft and florist shops and garden centers, this is used to mask foam blocks in arrangements formed in low containers.

Hairpin wire holders. These are specially designed for use in flower arrangements to hold stems in place. However, ordinary hairpins can usually be used to serve the same purpose.

Pincushions or needle points. These come in a variety of geometric shapes and sizes and are placed on the bottom of a container and used to hold flower stems in place. Several of these will come in handy for your arrangements.

Containers for Indoor Arrangements

If a container is attractive and it can hold water—or something can be put inside of it that will hold water—it can be used for live flower arrangements. However, some containers are better suited to arrangements than others.

When selecting a container, you will want to consider:

Shape. Containers come in all shapes—shallow bowls, cylinders, compotes, goblets, urns. For a display which makes a statement, round, oval, or rectangular shallow bowls should be ten to twelve inches in diameter or seven by fourteen inches, both about three inches deep. Tall containers should be ten to twelve inches high. The trumpet-beaker shaped vase, which flares out at the top, is best for most standard arrangements, since the cut-flower material is not squeezed into a bunch, but rather assumes its natural growing shape in the vase.

Color. Neutral colors blend with most plant ma-terial, but the best colors to use are shades of green, woody tones, mustard, beige, tan, or rust. For pastel arrangements, pale rose or pink is particularly attractive. Solid-colored shallow bowls and ceramic cylinders are also useful, if they complement the colors you are using in the arrangement.

Sheen. Avoid metal containers with brilliant finishes such as polished copper or brass, for they tend to overpower an arrangement. Pewter and silver are suitable, since they are not overly brilliant unless highly polished.

Beyond these basic guidelines, use your imagination. Look around your house, in the cellar and in the attic, and you will probably find all kinds of container possibilities. And don't limit yourself to the conventional flower vase. In fact, anything that will hold water, and even things that are not waterproof, can be used.

Ceramic pottery, heirloom china pieces such as covered dishes, soup tureens, sauce or gravy boats, sugar bowls, and pitchers, all lend themselves to attractive arrangements. Silver epergnes, champagne buckets, various serving bowls, and coffee and tea services can also be used. Pottery, such as stoneware jugs are usable as are glass brandy snifters, vases, and ice buckets. Attractive cups and saucers can be used for miniature arrangements. Shaving mugs, pewter mugs, beer steins, martini pitchers, large wineglasses, and even attractive wastebaskets can also be used.

Antique coffeepots, old Dutch ovens or stewing pots, and other kitchen paraphernalia that will hold water are particularly charming when filled with fresh flowers. Some people collect antique coffee cans and other Pop art from an earlier time. These can also be used to contain flower arrangements. Old milk bottles and mason jars, particularly those with a blue tint, are also effective containers for arrangements.

But you needn't restrain yourself to containers that hold water, for you can always insert a plastic container in any sort of container. Large and small baskets, hatboxes, old wooden boxes, and even elegant jewelry boxes can serve to hold an arrangement.

Principles of Flower Arranging

Needless to say, rules were made to be broken, and this certainly holds true of flower arranging. As you become more sophisticated in your experience, you will undoubtedly want to experiment with different proportions, balance, colors, and so forth. However, if you are starting out and are relatively inexperienced, the following basic concepts and rules should help you in creating arrangements that are pleasing to the eye.

PROPORTION. It is easy to tell if your flower arrangement is in good proportion. If you use a tall vase, simply look at the finished arrangement. If the vase seems to be too tall for the arrangement, the proportion is wrong. As a rule of thumb, the height of the flower arrangement should extend above the rim of the vase one and a half to two times the height of the vase.

If you use a shallow, low container, the rule of thumb is that the height of the tallest stem in the arrangement should be equal to one and a half to two times the width or diameter of the bowl.

BALANCE. This term refers to the stability of an arrangement, that is, whether or not it appears to be lopsided. There are two kinds of balance, symmetrical and asymmetrical. Symmetrical balance means that when you look at an arrangement, the two halves are identical or nearly identical. Asymmetrical balance means that the two halves are not equal, but appear to have equal importance to the eye.

Achieving symmetrical balance is relatively sim-

Hosta, euphorbia, and aruncus fill this urn with a symmetrically balanced arrangement. Arrangement by Madame Walda Poiron.

ple. Simply try to make the two halves of the arrangement the same. Asymmetrical balance requires more experience, but the effect is far more interesting. Arrange the two sides differently, but be sure that both sides are of equal importance to the eye. You can do this in many ways. One way is to use a profusion of small, soft-colored blossoms on one side of the arrangement with a few large soft-colored blossoms on the other. Or you can arrange one side with several short, large, bright-colored blossoms, while the other side of the arrangement can contain many more taller bright-colored blossoms. Juxtapose tall and short, bright and muted, few and many blossoms, coarse and delicate textures and foliage types in the same way.

TEXTURE. Texture contrast is important in an arrangement and is easy to accomplish. Contrast nature's own textures, that is, combine flowers with soft, velvety petals, leaves with shiny foliage, flowers with coarse, ruffled petals, leaves with muted foliage, and so forth. Your cut-flower garden will provide you with an infinite variety of flower and foliage texture.

COLOR. In the same sense, color contrast is also important in an arrangement. Interesting arrangements are secured by combining hues of greater and lesser "value," or color intensity. Pale hues have less value than deep colors, which usually means that you use more of them in an arrangement in order to balance the darker colors. Dark colors look best in low arrangements, as they appear heavier to the eye.

The color wheel consists of the three primary colors—red, blue, and yellow—and the three secondary colors—purple, green, and orange.

They are placed this way around the wheel:

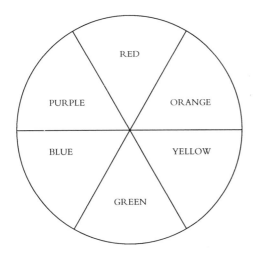

The secondary garden colors are adjacent to the primary colors on the wheel: Purple falls between primary red and blue, orange between red and yellow, and green between blue and yellow. If you mix any one primary color with another, the result is a secondary color. That is, if you mix red and blue pigment, you get purple; mix blue and yellow and you get green; mix yellow and red and you get orange.

These become accent colors when they are placed together with colors directly opposite them on the color wheel, that is, a primary color with the opposite secondary color. A visual impact occurs when red is used with green, orange with blue, and purple with yellow. Keep in mind that when a color red is specified, that means all its shades; for red that would include pink, carmine, scarlet, etc.

Here is a list of primary, secondary, and accent colors which you can refer to when creating arrangements.

When you plan the color scheme for your arrangement, if you select purple as your main color, concentrate on using the adjacent colors on the wheel, that is, blue and red, along with white when you select blossom color. This could include not only red but pink, and mauve, and not only blue, but lavender, light blue, deep blue, etc. An occasional accent can be provided by the opposite color on the wheel, that is, in this case, yellow, from pale to bright hues.

PRIMARY FLOWER COLOR	SECONDARY FLOWER COLORS	ACCENT COLOR
Red	Purple and orange	Green
Purple	Blue and red	Yellow
Blue	Purple and green	Orange
Green	Blue and Yellow	Red
Yellow	Green and orange	Purple
Orange	Yellow and red	Blue

In this lovely arrangement, white baby's breath has been effectively used to provide soft contrast to the deep pink zinnias and pale pink snapdragons. Arrangement by Ellen Kosciusko.

liage from a flower which you are not using in an arrangement to provide contrast of form, as well as texture.

FOCUS AND ACCENT. As in rooms and gardens, focal points in flower arrangements add interesting dimensions to the visual experience. You can achieve this by using a blossom of a contrasting or complementary color or perhaps a more intense hue of the same color if the arrangement is monochromatic. Sometimes foliage can also be used for focus or accent. In any case, be sure that you are subtle in your selection; if you aren't, the entire effect of an arrangement can be destroyed.

HARMONY OR UNITY. This should be your final goal

Here's living proof that bright-colored blossoms can be made to work in tandem effectively in flower arrangements. Arrangement by Jane Overman.

White flowers, as well as silver and gray foliage, should always be considered when creating arrangements. These colors offer interesting neutral tones which serve to subdue masses of bright-colored blossoms, or to highlight lesser numbers of the brighter flowers.

Again, all rules are made to be broken. If you feel like mixing what appear to be incongruous colors, go ahead. At least try it, and see if it works for you.

Although it may seem obvious, when designing an arrangement keep in mind that strong, pure colors offer a strong statement, one which may overwhelm the room or setting you wish to enhance. Pastel colors are more subtle and are usually more appropriate for most settings.

FORM. Contrast in form is also important. The chalice shape of a tulip combined with a pointed leaf form mutually enhance each other. Lacy leaves look more interesting if combined with solid-looking flower heads. Don't be afraid to substitute fo-

The Basics of Flower Arranging
· · ·37· · ·

To add dramatic height to this arrangement, wild Queen Anne's lace has been incorporated. Arrangement by Mable Brown.

Lines
Triangles (pyramids and cones)
Curves
Circles (spheres)
Angles

These can be further divided into:

Symmetrical triangles. These arrangements are well balanced and easy to create, and accommodate large numbers of flowers of different colors, as well as foliage and dried material. The Victorians were particularly fond of this shape.

Asymmetrical triangle. This shape accommodates a major focal point quite well. If there is one particular blossom you wish to feature, this form will work well. The shape is rather chic, stylish, and grand when the arrangement is tall and loosely created.

Line arrangements. These offer a stylized oriental look, such as the Japanese ikebana style, so popular in contemporary decor.

Angle arrangements. Actually, this form is a scalene triangle, one with the three sides of different lengths. It is very versatile and accommodates a wide range of different textured and colored blossoms.

Round forms. Thee are usually used for table centerpieces and accommodate a wide variety of flower textures and colors. A round arrangement is quite straightforward and easy to create.

Cone forms. This form is a spin-off of the symmetrical triangle, with a round bowl. Although somewhat formal, this shape can be softened by using loosely formed blossoms.

Crescents, curves, and s-curves. These are probably the most adventurous shapes which you can undertake in designing your arrangements. They offer a lot of latitude and can be quite challenging to the

in creating an arrangement. If you skillfullly combine blossoms, foliage, and container and then set the arrangement in the right location, you will create a harmonious picture in your home.

The Different Kinds of Shapes in Arrangements

Now that you have learned about basic design principles and color use, it is time to consider the different classic shapes that can be used in flower arrangements. These shapes are based on three-dimensional geometric forms. These are:

The designer has used at least eight different kinds of flowers in creating this arrangement in a symmetrical triangular form. Notice how the colors of the flowers repeat the colors in the elegant vase. Arrangement by Jane Overman.

hobbyist; they work well in contemporary settings.

Torch forms. This shape emphasizes the perpendicular line, with the arrangement in the shape of a torch. It is particularly effective placed in an area where you wish to inject height.

Convex curves. This is very suitable for table centerpiece arrangements, and somewhat more interesting in terms of shape than the round form.

Dressing Up Arrangements with Foliage

When designing any arrangement try to include foliage. Foliage serves to set off the flowers you select, to add interesting lines to an arrangement, and to fill out the bottom of an arrangement which has been placed in dry foam blocks.

For example, although the jade green straplike

foliage of daffodils is certainly a handsome addition to a simple daffodil bouquet, if you include some broad-leaved evergreen foliage, the daffodils will be very dramatically set off. Foliage of silver or gray coloration, feathery textures, variegated yellow-and-green of white-and-green foliage all add original-looking touches to arrangements. Simple cut flowers purchased at the florist can be "fleshed out" with lush evergreen foliage in the winter, or with autumn leaves in the fall.

Beyond setting off and filling out the arrangement, think in terms of lines. Long branches of arching forsythia and other spring foliage, even after the flowers have faded and the leaves have emerged, add graceful lines to any arrangement. Spearlike iris foliage adds interesting shapes to late spring and summer creations. Look around your garden and experiment with different textured and shaped foliage. The result will most often remove an arrangement from the ordinary into the very special.

Rejuvenating Arrangements

When you create an arrangement using several different types of flowers, the vase life of each may well differ. For example, in creating a fall arrangement, suppose that you decide to include Japanese anemones with chrysanthemums. The vase life of Japanese anemones is only four to six days, while chrysanthemums may well last from two to three weeks. There is no need to toss out the entire arrangement just because some of the flowers included are "over the hill." Simply remove the spent flowers and toss them out. Recut and recondition the remaining flowers (see page 13), thoroughly clean the container, refill with water and additive if recommended, add more fresh flowers if desired, and rearrange the remaining flowers.

Getting to Work

Of course, you will need a place to work. Ideally, the best place to prepare and condition cut flowers and to create arrangements is a potting bench with a large work surface, shelves on which you can store containers and other arranging paraphernalia, and a source of water nearby. If you have the space, and it is close to a water supply, say in an attached garage, cellar, enclosed porch, or spare room, an inexpensive bench and shelves can be installed. Or, in lieu of that, a large table and an old bookshelf will do.

However, few of us are fortunate enough to have the luxury of this extra space. Any large surface, a kitchen table or kitchen counter, can be used as a work area, as long as it is close to a water supply. It is a good idea to keep all of your containers and arranging supplies together, so that when you are ready to create arrangements, you don't have to go looking all over the house for these things. Any cupboard, or even several large boxes which can be stored away, will hold almost everything you'll need.

6

The Quick and Easy
Cut-flower Collection

. . .

Annuals

Annual flowering plants are indispensable for creating near instant gratification in your cut-flower garden. They live only for one season, growing from seed, flowering, and completing their life cycle in this short span of time. With a minimal amount of care, they provide an abundance of spectacular cut-flower material, all for the price of a few packages of seeds or six-pack containers of young plants.

Study the entries that follow and decide which annuals are appropriate for your needs. Then send for some of the seed catalogs listed in Sources. Do this in January or February.

HOW TO BUY ANNUALS. There are two ways you can buy annuals. First, you can purchase six-packs of plants at garden centers and nurseries. This is the surest way to secure almost instant color in your garden. It is also the way to get annuals that must be started indoors under lights long before outdoor planting time in order to ensure bloom by summer. Beyond that, if you are busy and don't have the time to plant seeds, water, and care for them in their seedling stage, ready-grown annuals, although more expensive than a package of seeds, are the answer. However, there are drawbacks to six-pack offerings. Although more and more varieties become available every year, the industry still offers little more than about a dozen cultivars in a dozen or so varieties of each, and these the most common annuals grown.

The other way to grow annuals is to purchase seeds and grow them yourself. Whether you purchase seeds from seed racks in supermarkets, garden centers, or nurseries or buy them from mail-order houses, a much larger variety of plants is available to you. However, and here's the hitch: some plants require a much longer time to germinate and grow to flowering stage. Since the seeds of many kinds of annuals should not be planted outdoors until after danger of frost, some will not bloom until very late in the summer, if then.

And beyond that, some seeds need to be sprinkled on the soil surface because they require light to germinate, and must be kept evenly moist at all times, an undertaking which can become tiresome.

So, if you wish to sow seeds directly into the ground, you must limit yourself to those varieties which can be planted outdoors early in spring and sustain late frosts, those which will grow to flowering stage quickly if planted outdoors after all danger of frost, and, unless you have the time and inclination to provide evenly moist conditions for surface-sown seeds, those which should be covered with soil when planted.

Even with these restrictions, there are scores of varieties which you can successfully bring to flower by sowing directly in the soil either in early spring or after frost.

It is a simple matter to avail yourself of annuals which do need a head start indoors. If you have a window with a southern exposure, you can place trays of seeds on shelves in the windows or on a

Charlotte Ford's large annual cutting garden in Southampton, New York, provides all the flowers she needs for summer entertaining.

The Cut-flower Garden
· · ·42· · ·

table in front of it. Though you will have some-success, the daylight hours are not really long enough to start strong, vigorous seedlings in mid-winter and early spring in this manner. A far better way to start seedlings indoors is to install a simple fluorescent light structure to start seeds. With a small investment of time and money, new worlds of plant adventure will open up to you. You can build a reasonable-size structure for about one quarter the cost of a small manufactured unit.

BUILDING AN INEXPENSIVE SEED-STARTING LIGHT UNIT. Purchase a four-foot long industrial fluorescent light fixture. They cost about fifteen dollars in most home improvement centers. The fixtures usually come with lights, both cool tubes. Substitute one warm tube for one of the cool tubes. There is no need to buy expensive, special plant-growing fluorescent tubes. Despite manufacturer's claims, the results for starting seedlings are just about equally as good using one cool and one warm tube. Either hang the fixture in a heated basement over a table or workbench, or attach it to the bottom of a shelf in the house. Plug it in and you are ready to start seeds indoors.

Since fixtures should remain on for about fourteen hours a day, you may want to buy a timer switch to turn the lights off and on if you don't wish to be bothered with this daily task. These cost less than ten dollars. You can start with one fixture, though even at the beginning you will find that you will want at least two. And after several years, you will undoubtedly find that you want three or four to accommodate all the plants you wish to start from seed.

STARTING SEEDS UNDER LIGHTS. You can sow seeds in just about any container imaginable: milk cartons, plastic containers, flowerpots, aluminum trays, in short, anything that will hold a seed-starting soil mixture. Be advised that you need drainage, so if you use homemade containers, poke holes through the bottoms so that excess water can escape. Beyond the homemade, there are many products available in garden centers and nurseries which are made specifically for starting seeds.

Every now and then, however, something comes on the market which is so exceptional, so easy to use, and which results in such total success that it is worth investigating. If you wish to start seeds indoors under lights, it will be well worth your time to write to Gardener's Supply Co., 128 Intervale Road, Burlington, VT 05401, (800) 863-1700. They have a seed-starting kit called Accelerated Propagation System or APS, which is made of Styrofoam. Included is a reservoir arrangement and a felt capillary matting, which absorbs water and irrigates seed flats from below. This cuts down tremendously on the watering process. The trays hold about three to four quarts of water, and once filled can be checked perhaps once a week to see if they need refilling. Seedlings are watered from the bottom, so they are not damaged by the force of top watering. A clear plastic top is included to create a mini-greenhouse, assuring that humidity is maintained. They cost around thirteen dollars, plus shipping.

These units are a godsend to the busy gardener, and the results are impressive. One achieves almost 100 percent germination from seeds planted in them. They are very reasonable in price, can be reused again and again during the season as well as year in and year out, and are also useful for rooting cuttings, watering houseplants when you are away from home, in short, absolutely indispensable to the home gardener. A four-foot industrial fluorescent light fixture will accommodate three of these self-watering seed-starter trays.

Although you will have to invest some money in setting up an indoor light system, consider that a package of six annual plants costs about three dollars these days. Each of the APS units contains twenty-four or forty spaces for growing plants, depending on which one you buy. If you start with three, you can grow 120 plants. These same plants would cost you around sixty dollars at nurseries and garden centers. Quite a substantial savings indeed, especially when you consider that you can reuse these year in and year out. In addition, you will have the pleasure of watching seedlings grow during the late winter and early spring months.

So then, whether you use makeshift containers or avail yourself of the starter units, the only other thing you will need to start seeds indoors is the proper soil. Do not purchase potting soil, as it is too heavy in texture to start seeds. Terra-lite or Reddi-Mix, available in garden centers and nurseries, are two products mixed to provide perfect growing conditions for starting seeds. They are sterilized and include vermiculite to lighten the soil and retain moisture. Before placing these products in a container, moisten them thoroughly. Then plant the seeds according to instructions on the packet, that is, either lightly covered with soil or on the soil's surface. If you are using a seed starting unit that you purchased, plant several seeds in each individual compartment. Insert labels in the proper places. Place under lights for fourteen hours a day with the soil surface about two inches from the light tube surface. If you are using a homemade container, mist with room temperature water, using a mister available in garden centers and nurseries, until the soil is evenly moist. When seedlings sport a second pair of leaves, thin out all but the strongest in each compartment of your seed-starting kit.

If you use the APS unit, the reservoir will provide the proper amount of water. Whatever type of container you're using, feed with an all-purpose liquid houseplant fertilizer at one quarter the strength recommended by the manufacturer once a week. About one week before outdoor planting time (this date varies from location to location throughout the country; however, if plants are to be set out after "all danger of frost," check locally to find out when it is safe to plant tomatoes out-

doors—planting time for these annuals will be the same), you must "harden off" your plants. This acclimates them to the strong sunlight and cool nights of outdoor growing. You do this by placing the containers outdoors in a shady spot during the day and bringing them indoors at night. After two days of this, place them in a sunny spot for about half a day and a shady spot for the other half; the next day leave them in the sun for the entire day and bring them indoors only if the night is going to be chilly. In any event, if it rains bring them indoors. If the leaves start to look bleached, they are getting too much sun and are not yet accustomed to the strong light. Move them back into the shade. After about one week, you can safely plant them in your garden where you want them.

SELECTING A SITE. Most annuals prefer full sun, so if you are installing a large bed or border, select a sunny location. Consult the individual entries to see which kinds of annuals are suitable for the various light conditions. Since most annuals are not fussy about soil, this should not be a problem, but many will resent very wet conditions, such as boggy areas, or places on your property where water sits for a day or so after rain.

PLANNING THE ANNUAL GARDEN. As always, work out your planting on graph paper. Use a scale of an inch to every one foot of garden space, and sketch out the area you wish to plant. Be adventurous, for annual plantings are installed for one season only, they aren't permanent.

You might want to try both a border and an island bed, to decide which is best for your property. In planning a border, if you limit yourself to plants which grow about two feet high, a three- or four-foot-wide border will be suitable. If you wish to grow taller varieties of plants, those which grow from two to six feet or taller, the minimum width of the border should be eight feet. Free-form island beds containing taller varieties should be about eight feet across at their widest point. The bed

This lovely French-style parterre garden is filled with annual forget-me-nots and pansies, both suitable for spring mini-arrangements.

should be about three times as long as it is wide. If medium height and low-growing plants are what you wish to install, a five- or six-foot-wide island bed is suitable.

In a border, place the tall plants in the rear, medium height plants in the middle, and low-growing varieties in front. In an island bed, taller plants go in the middle, then medium height plants, with low-growing plants around the edge.

Plant in groups of five or seven if you are installing a bed or border. Even numbers of plants tend to look like blocks of foliage and color in the garden. Also, avoid planting in straight lines or in circles around trees, birdbaths, or shrubs. The effect looks ridiculous.

When you are ready to install your annual border or bed, take your chart to the garden with you along with a ruler to measure the spacing of plants. As a rule, tall-growing plants should be spaced two feet apart, medium-height plants eighteen inches apart, and low-growing plants twelve inches apart, with dwarf miniatures around six inches apart.

PREPARING THE SOIL. Most annuals are not fussy about soil; however, working the soil to a depth of about one foot helps assure success. If your soil is overly sandy, or heavy clay, mix in well-rotted compost or sphagnum peat moss at a ratio of about one part additive to two parts soil. The compost or peat moss will help retain moisture during dry spells and make it easier for a healthy root system to form. When you have prepared the planting site, water thoroughly.

WHEN TO PLANT ANNUALS. Most annuals are planted after all danger of frost is past. However, there are a few, sweet peas and larkspur, for example, which can be planted in early spring, as soon as the ground is workable. Check the individual entries for further information.

HOW TO PLANT ANNUALS. First check the entries to see if the varieties you are planting require rich soil, in which case work into the soil about one tablespoon of all-purpose 5-10-5 fertilizer per square foot of garden space. Be advised that most annuals do not require rich soil and feeding may be unnecessary. Then dig a hole large enough to contain the small rootball, set the plant in, firm the soil around the plant, and water thoroughly. As explained above, when you plant annuals from seed, some require light to germinate, in which case they must be sowed on the soil surface, and others require dark, in which case they should be covered with a light coating of soil. Seed packages always contain the exact instructions about depth of planting, whether or not to cover with soil, spacing of initial planting, and thinning instructions. Read them and follow them for best results.

MULCHING. It is a good idea to lay down a one- or two-inch layer of mulch. Use shredded pine or cedar bark or compost as mulch. In this way, weeding will be almost eliminated, moisture will be retained, and the bed will look tidy.

MAINTENANCE. Annual plantings are to a great extent maintenance-free. Pests and diseases rarely attack, and, if you mulch, weeds will be smothered. However, one thing you must do is deadhead spent blooms. That means removing flowers which have faded. The reason for this is not just for aesthetics but to extend the period of bloom. The purpose of flowers is to create seeds, to regenerate themselves. Once seeds have formed, the plant has accomplished its purpose, and will stop flowering. By deadheading you frustrate this process and keep the plant blooming until frost.

WATERING. Although many annuals are drought resistant, for best results a good deep watering once a week during periods of summer drought is recommended. Water so that the ground is soaked to a depth of about one foot.

PESTS AND DISEASES. Mercifully, most annuals are pest and disease resistant, if not totally free of these problems. However, there are a few problems which may require care. If your plants do not look healthy, inspect them carefully to determine what may be the problem. It is a good idea to bring a magnifying glass to the garden with you to expedite diagnosis. Here are a few problems which you may encounter.

Aphids. These small green, black, pink, yellow, or red, soft-bodied insects attack almost all plants. If plants are stunted and leaves deformed, aphids may be present. Spray regularly with malathion, according to the manufacturer's directions. If you wish to use a natural repellent, spray with rotenone, according to the manufacturer's directions, or with a solution of half water, half detergent.

Lace bugs. Small bugs with large lacy wings that attack azaleas, hawthorn, and other plants. If plants are under siege, leaves will appear mottled. Spray regularly with malathion, according to the manufacturer's directions. If you wish to use a natural repellent, spray with rotenone or pyrethrum according to the manufacturer's directions.

Leafhoppers. Wedge-shaped insects that hop and attack many plants. They may cause leaves to turn pale or brown, and growth will be stunted. Malathion is the chemical spray to use, pyrethrum the botanical spray.

Mealybugs. These white cottony insects attack many plants, causing them to become stunted. Sevin is the chemical spray to use and although not as effective, spraying daily with a half-and-half solution of water and detergent for a week may help.

Mildew. This is a mold which forms on the foliage of some plants, particularly zinnias, monarda, deciduous azaleas, and phlox. To combat this, spray regularly from midsummer to fall with Captan or Benomyl, available at garden centers and nurseries, according to manufacturer's instructions.

Mites. These are minute sucking insects that attack almost all plants. They will cause leaves to discolor. Sevin is the chemical spray to use. If you wish to use a natural repellent, spraying daily with a half-and-half solution of water and detergent for about a week may help.

Red spiders. One of many varieties of mites which might strike. A plant under siege will become yellow and weak and the undersides of its leaves dirty-looking, the result of soil sticking to the fine webs the mites weave. Webs will first appear near the ribs or margins of leaves and then cover the entire surface. Larger mites can be seen with the naked eye. Spray with malathion. Although not as effective, spraying with a half-and-half solution of water and detergent may help. Usually red spiders do not attack until the heat of summer.

Scale. These tiny, usually hard, oval insects may attack many plants, causing leaves to yellow and drop. Scale is difficult to control; however, spraying in late winter with dormant oil spray should smother insects. Or in lieu of that, spraying with a half-and-half solution of water and detergent may help.

Snails and slugs. Easily recognized and easily cured, these nasty molluscs attack many plants, eating the foliage. Set a shallow aluminum pie plate filled with beer near the plants being attacked. Slugs love beer, will climb into the pie plate, and drown.

Thrips. These tiny, winged insects cause leaves to become silvery. The chemical cure is malathion, the botanical spray is rotenone.

Aster, China
(Callistephus chinensis)

Color: Red, pink, purple, blue, white.

Description: Double, pompon-, and ball-shaped blossoms which range from miniature to 6″ across held over handsome, deep green, notched, ovate-shaped foliage.

Height: 6 to 30″.

Soil: Rich. Fortify with compost, rotted manure, or 5-10-5 fertilizer at the rate of one tablespoon per square foot.

Light: Full sun, but partial shade will extend blooming period of individual blossoms.

Moisture: Moderately moist.

Planting time: Start indoors under lights six weeks before danger of frost is over in your area, March 15 to 30 in most parts of the country.

Growing season care: Deadhead for continuous bloom.

Bloom time: Late summer to killing frost.

Length of bloom: 2 months.

Live arrangements: Yes.

Vase life: 8 to 14 days.

Drying: No.

Tips: One of the most popular of all annuals, good for fall gardens. 'Super Giants' are the large, 6-inch blossoms and 'Early Pompon Serene' are about 2 inches in diameter; both offer a bonanza of cutting material. Avoid planting asters in the same place two years in a row, as they will not thrive the second year.

Cockscomb
(Celosia plumosa, C. cristata)

Color: Brilliant red, orange, apricot, yellow, fuchsia.

Description: Blossoms of *C. plumosa* are feathery and velvety, while those of *C. cristata* are crested

Celosia plumosa can be used in both fresh and dried arrangements.

Cornflower or Bachelor's Button
(*Centaurea cyanus*)

Color: Blue, pink, white, maroon.
Description: Thistlelike flowers in close heads on silver-green foliage.
Height: 2 to 2½′.
Soil: Ordinary.
Light: Full sun.
Moisture: Moderately moist.
Planting time: Seedlings resist early spring cold. Sow seed in the place you wish to grow them about 4 weeks before it is time to set out tomatoes in your area.

Pink bachelor's buttons combine well with the traditional blue variety.

and velvety. Foliage of both is medium green.
Height: 9″ to 2′.
Soil: Well-drained, light, rich.
Light: Full sun.
Moisture: Drought resistant, but water regularly during extended summer drought.
Planting time: Sow in situ, after all danger of frost. Thin to about 1′ apart.
Growing season care: Deadhead for rebloom.
Bloom time: Midsummer to killing frost.
Length of bloom: 3 to 4 months.
Live arrangements: Yes.
Vase life: 2 to 3 weeks.
Drying: Yes. Hang dry.
Tips: Many gardeners consider celosia garish, and the colors can be overwhelming in a garden, so consider this if you decide to grow this unusual plant.

Growing season care: Deadhead for continuous bloom.

Bloom time: June to September.

Length of bloom: 3 to 4 months.

Live arrangements: Yes.

Vase life: 5 to 7 days.

Drying: Yes. Hang dry or silica dry.

Tips: Very easy to grow. 'Ultra Dwarf Blue' is a compact version of this popular favorite. If you fail to deadhead after bloom, plant will bloom itself to death and become unsightly by midsummer.

Cosmos

Color: Bright clear red, rose, pink, yellow, white, crimson.

Description: Daisy-shaped blossoms on feathery foliage.

Height: 3 to 6'.

Soil: Ordinary, well-drained.

Light: Full sun.

Moisture: Moderately moist.

Planting time: Outdoors, after all danger of frost.

Growing season care: Deadhead for continuous bloom.

Bloom time: Early summer to killing frost.

Bloom time: 4 to 5 months.

Live arrangements: Yes.

Vase life: 5 to 7 days.

Drying: No.

Tips: Useful in the loose informal arrangements so popular today. Many new exciting varieties have been introduced recently. 'Daydream' is particularly profuse and quite lovely. To encourage branching and thus more flowers, pinch the tips of the plants when they are 1' high, and then again when 18" high. Cosmos reseed readily, but do not become a nuisance. Birds are attracted to cosmos.

Dusty Miller

(Senecio maritima)

Color: Stunning silver foliage.

Description: Compact, moundlike growth habit. No flowers.

Height: 8 to 12".

Soil: Ordinary, well-drained.

Light: Full sun.

Moisture: Drought resistant, but for best results, water regularly throughout growing season.

Planting time: Start indoors under lights 6 weeks before danger of frost is over in your area, March 15 to 30 in most parts of the country.

In recent years, cosmos have become very popular with flower arrangers. Their feathery foliage is used along with the blossoms.

Growing season care: Remove spent foliage.
Bloom time: Early summer to killing frost.
Length of bloom: 5 to 6 months.
Live arrangements: Yes.
Vase life: 1 to 2 weeks.
Drying: Yes. Hang dry.
Tips: Very useful in arrangements for silver foliage contrast. 'Silver Dust' is a compact variety with fernlike silvery white foliage. Easier to grow than perennial silver-leaved artemisia and accomplishes the same purpose in arrangements. Winters over in milder areas of the country.

Forget-Me-Not
(Myosotis sylvatica)

Color: Blue, with some pink and white varieties.
Description: Tiny clusters of blossoms on medium green, dainty foliage.
Height: 8 to 12 ".
Soil: Well-drained.
Light: Partial shade.
Moisture: Moderately moist.
Planting time: Outdoors, in situ, after all danger of frost.
Growing season care: Deadhead for continuous bloom.
Bloom time: Late spring through early summer.
Length of bloom: 3 to 4 months.
Live arrangements: Yes.
Vase life: 3 to 5 days.
Drying: No.
Tips: Often self-sows once established.

Heliotrope
(Heliotropus)

Color: Deep purple.
Description: 8 to 12" wide clusters of florets held on compact, bushy plants.

Height: 8 to 10".
Soil: Rich, well-drained.
Light: Full sun.
Moisture: Moderately moist.
Planting time: Start indoors under lights 6 to 8 weeks before danger of frost is over in your area, March 1 to 15 in most parts of the country.
Growing season care: Deadhead for continuous bloom.
Bloom time: Midsummer to killing frost.
Length of bloom: 3 to 4 months.
Live arrangements: Yes.
Vase life: 5 to 7 days.
Drying: Yes. Silica dry.
Tips: This old-fashioned favorite is highly fragrant. 'Marine' is large flowering. A bouquet will scent an entire room. Strangely enough, it is rarely grown in American gardens.

Larkspur or Annual Delphinium
(Consolida ambigua, syn. Delphinium ajacis)

Color: Blue, red, white, pink, purple.
Description: Spikes of florets held over medium green foliage.
Height: 3 to 4'.
Soil: Moderately rich, well-drained soil. Compost or well-rotted manure worked in helps them attain maximum growth and flower display.
Light: Full sun.
Moisture: Moderately moist.
Planting time: Seedlings resist early spring cold. Sow seed in the place you wish them to grow as soon as ground is workable, or sow them in the fall. They will winter over and germinate in the early spring.
Growing season care: Deadhead for continuous bloom.

Bloom time: Midsummer.

Length of bloom: 4 to 6 weeks.

Live arrangements: Yes.

Vase life: 6 to 10 days.

Drying: Yes. Hang dry or silica dry.

Tips: Seeds will not germinate in warm weather. Easy to grow. In late spring larkspur can be used in arrangements in place of delphiniums which are much more difficult to grow. The 'Imperial' strain is recommended. Self-sows in most areas.

WARNING: *If you use this for indoor arrangements, keep in mind that the young foliage and stems of the plant are poisonous to dogs, cats, and human beings if eaten and can be fatal!*

Marigold
(Tagetes)

Color: Gold, yellow, orange, white, maroon.

Description: Single or double pompom-shaped blossoms from 1 to 6″ in diameter, depending on variety, on handsome deep green foliage.

Height: 6″ to 4′.

Soil: Ordinary.

Light: Full sun, but will bloom in partial shade.

Moisture: Moderately moist.

Planting time: Outdoors, after all danger of frost.

Growing season care: Deadhead for continuous bloom.

Bloom time: Early summer to killing frost.

Length of bloom: 3 to 4 months.

Live arrangements: Yes.

Vase life: 7 to 14 days.

Drying: Yes. Silica dry.

Tips: Many find the odor of marigolds offensive. A simple solution is to place about one tablespoon of sugar in the vase water. The odor will be substantially diminished. Hundreds of varieties are available.

Marigold, Pot
(Calendula officinalis)

Color: Yellow, gold, orange-apricot, cream.

Description: 2″ wide, single and double daisylike blossoms, on straplike, medium green, fuzzy foliage.

Height: 2′.

Soil: Ordinary.

Light: Full sun.

Moisture: Moderately moist.

Planting time: Seedlings resist early spring cold. Sow seed in the place you wish to grow them about 4 weeks before it is time to set out tomatoes in your area, around April 1 in most areas.

Growing season care: Deadhead for continuous bloom.

Bloom time: Early summer to killing frost.

Length of bloom: 3 to 4 months.

Live arrangements: Yes.

Vase life: 6 to 14 days.

Drying: Yes. Hang dry or silica dry.

Tips: Easy to grow. Flowers are edible and add an attractive touch to salads. Since they are similar in appearance to some marigolds and since their odor is not offensive, many prefer to use calendulas in arrangements instead of marigolds. For medium-size and large arrangements, the taller-growing 'Pacific' varieties are best.

Pansy
(Viola × wittrockiana)

Color: White, blue, purple, mahogany, coral, peach, orange, black, rose, apricot, yellow, bicolored.

Description: Familiar blossoms on deep green, glossy foliage.

Height: 4 to 9″.

Soil: Rich, well-drained, high in organic matter.

Light: Full sun, but will grow in semishade.

Moisture: Prefers moist conditions, so keep well-watered and mulch to keep roots cool.

Planting time: As soon as ground is workable in spring.

Planting instructions: Set plants at soil level about one foot apart.

Growing season care: Deadhead for continuous bloom.

Bloom time: Early spring to early summer. Heat of summer diminishes bloom and often kills plant.

Live arrangements: Yes.

Vase life: 3 to 6 days.

Drying: Yes. Use microwave method.

Tips: It is best to purchase six-packs of plants in early spring at local garden centers and nurseries. For arrangements, pick when blossoms are fully open.

Pinks
(Dianthus chinensis)

and Carnations
(D. caryophyllus)

Color: Brilliant-colored scarlet, salmon, white, yellow, pink, crimson.

Description: Pompom-shaped blossoms on attractive silver-green foliaged plants.

Height: Pinks range from 8 to 12″, carnations 12 to 36″.

Soil: Well-drained, average.

Light: Full sun.

Moisture: Moderately moist.

Planting time: Outdoors, after all danger of frost.

Growing season care: Deadhead for continuous bloom.

Bloom time: Midsummer to killing frost.

Length of bloom: 3 to 4 months.

Live arrangements: Yes.

Vase life: 7 to 12 days.

Drying: Yes. Silica dry.

Tips: Pinks are an old-fashioned flower still as popular as ever in arrangements. Its clove fragrance is very evocative. If you plant annual carnations (*D. caryophyllus*), don't expect them to grow anywhere near as large as the greenhouse-growth florist version.

Sage
(Salvia)

Color: Brilliant red, purple.

Description: Spikes of florets on handsome dark green foliage.

Height: 1½ to 4′.

Soil: Ordinary with good drainage.

Light: Full sun.

Moisture: Moderately moist.

Planting time: Outdoors, after all danger of frost.

Planting instructions: Surface sow. Do not cover seeds with soil or planting medium since light is needed for germination.

Growing season care: Deadhead for continuous bloom.

Bloom time: Midsummer to killing frost.

Length of bloom: 3 to 4 months.

Live arrangements: Yes.

Vase life: 5 to 7 days.

Drying: No.

Tips: When plants are 3 to 4″ high, pinch the tops to encourage branching and more flowers. Since the color of most annual salvia is a vivid, garish bright red, it is perhaps best not to try to include it in a border or bed planting but to place it in a cut-flower garden. If bright red is called for in an arrangement, you can't miss this one. The beautiful purple salvia 'Victoria', however, is appropriate in almost any garden.

Snapdragon
(Antirrhinum)

Color: All colors except true blue.

Description: Spikes of single, double, and butter-fly-shaped flowers on attractive dark green, bushy foliage.

Height: 6 to 8″ for dwarf varieties, to 5′ for some standard varieties.

Soil: Rich, well-drained.

Light: Full sun, but will tolerate some shade.

Moisture: Moderately moist.

Planting time: Start indoors under lights 8 weeks before danger of frost is over in your area, March 1 to 15 in most parts of the country.

Planting instructions: Surface sow. Do not cover seeds with planting medium since light is needed for germination.

Growing season care: Deadhead for continuous bloom.

Bloom time: Early summer to killing frost and beyond.

Length of bloom: 4 to 5 months.

Live arrangements: Yes.

Vase life: 6 to 12 days.

Drying: Yes. Silica dry.

Tips: The Rocket hybrids are ideal for cutting. Pinch tips of plants when about 3″ tall to encourage branching. Then pinch again when new shoots are about three inches tall. Snapdragons often winter over in moderate climates. Usually the second year's bloom is even more spectacular than the first.

Spider Plant
(Cleome)

Color: Rose, pink, lilac, purple, white.

Description: Large spiderlike blossoms set on lobed foliage.

Cleome is another old-fashioned flower which is enjoying renewed popularity.

Height: 3 to 6′.

Soil: Light, sandy loam.

Light: Full sun.

Moisture: Moderately moist.

Planting time: Seedlings resist early spring cold. Sow seed in the place you wish them to grow about 4 weeks before it is time to set out tomatoes in your area.

Planting instructions: Surface sow. Do not cover seeds with planting medium since light is needed for germination.

Growing season care: Deadhead for continuous bloom.

Bloom time: Early summer to killing frost.

Length of bloom: 3 to 4 months.

Live arrangements: Yes.

Vase life: 5 to 7 days.

Drying: No.

Tips: Easy to grow. Although stems grow tall, they are quite sturdy and rarely need staking. They also sport thorns, so be careful. The sap exuded from stems is rarely a nuisance except when cutting.

Zinnia

Color: All colors except blue.

Description: Showy, prolific blooms ranging from miniature to giant make this one of the most utilitarian of annuals. Foliage is deep green and handsome.

Height: 8″ to 4′.

Soil: Ordinary.

Light: Full sun.

Moisture: Moderately moist. Because susceptible to powdery mildew, water early in the day so that excess moisture on foliage will evaporate.

Planting time: Outdoors, after all danger of frost.

Growing season care: Deadhead for continuous bloom.

Bloom time: Midsummer to killing frost.

Length of bloom: 3 to 4 months.

Live arrangements: Yes.

Vase life: 7 to 14 days.

Drying: Yes. Silica dry.

Tips: When seedlings are 4 inches high, pinch tips to encourage branching and more flowers. Zinnia foliage is prone to mildew, which can make plants look unsightly. To prevent this, spray from early summer to frost with Captan or Benomyl fungicides, available at garden centers and nurseries, according to manufacturer's instructions. *A better solution is to plant only the newly hybridized varieties which resist mildew.* Some of these are 'Yellow Marvel' and the Ruffles hybrids.

Everlastings

This name is given to a group of flowering annuals, biennials, and perennials which dry particularly well and are very useful in creating dried arrangements. See pages 25–31 for instructions on drying. All everlasting species—annual, biennial, and perennial—are included in this section. Very often these dried flowers are available for purchase in flower shops, nurseries, and even in supermarkets in the fall.

Although well suited to drying, all of the everlastings included here can also be used in fresh flower arrangements. And, when used this way, they are particularly long-lasting.

Bells of Ireland
(Moluccella laevis)

Plant type: Annual.

Color: Greenish yellow.

Description: Spikes of bell-shaped florets over medium green foliage.

Height: 2 to 3′.

Soil: Well-drained, average.

Light: Full sun.

Moisture: Drought resistant.

Planting time: For early bloom, start indoors under lights 8 weeks before last frost, March 1 in most parts of the country, or sow outdoors in situ after all danger of frost.

Bloom time: Early summer to killing frost.

Length of bloom: 3 to 4 months.

Live arrangements: Yes.

Vase life: 7 to 14 days.

Drying: Yes. Hang dry.

Tips: Very unusual and rare green-colored blossoms add exotic touches to dried arrangements. Harvest flowers for drying in late summer or early fall.

Chinese Lantern
(Physalis solanaceae)

Plant type: Perennial.

USDA zones: 3 to 9.

Color: Bright orange.

Description: Familiar lantern-shaped blossoms on medium green foliage.

Height: 2'.

Soil: Well-drained.

Light: Full sun.

Moisture: Drought resistant.

Planting time: Early spring for plants, but grows easily from seed.

Planting instructions: Surface sow in situ, after all danger of frost.

Growing season care: Cut foliage to the ground after harvesting the orange lantern fruits for drying.

Bloom time: Early fall to killing frost and beyond.

Length of bloom: 4 to 8 weeks.

Live arrangements: No.

Drying: Yes. Hang dry.

Tips: This is the great old-fashioned favorite, but can be invasive. Cut at end of season for drying.

Globe Amaranth
(Gomphrena)

Plant type: Annual.

Color: Brilliant red ('Strawberry Fields') and lavender ('Lavender Lady').

Description: 1″ pompons on medium green foliage.

Height: 2'.

Soil: Well-drained, average.

Light: Full sun.

Moisture: Drought resistant.

Planting time: For early bloom, start indoors under lights 8 weeks before last frost, March 1 in most parts of the country, or sow outdoors in situ

Here globe amaranth enhances purple Salvia 'Victoria' *in the garden, and can be used in fresh arrangements or dried for fall or winter use.*

after all danger of frost.

Bloom time: Early summer to killing frost.

Length of bloom: 3 to 4 months.

Live arrangements: Yes.

Vase life: 5 to 7 days.

Drying: Yes. Hang dry.

Tips: Harvest flowers for drying in late summer or early fall. 'Strawberry Fields' and 'Lavender Lady' are recent introductions, surpassing standard varieties in blossom size and abundance.

Honesty or Money Plant
(Lunaria)

Plant type: Biennial.

Color: Silver.

Description: 2″ round, flat silvery pods on jade green foliage.

Height: 30″.

Soil: Ordinary.

Light: Full sun.

Moisture: Drought resistant, but water regularly during prolonged summer drought.

Planting time: Early spring. Since honesty is a biennial, sow in early spring where you want it to grow for bloom the following year. May also bloom the same year.

Growing season care: At end of season, cut foliage to the ground. Will grow again following spring.

Bloom time: Late summer to killing frost.

Length of bloom: 2 to 3 months.

Live arrangements: No.

Drying: Yes. Hang dry.

Tips: Can take over a garden, so be sure to pull unwanted seedlings each spring.

Statice
(Limonium)

Plant type: Annual.

Color: Apricot, rose, purple, deep blue, light blue, white-yellow.

Description: Sprays of florets on medium green foliage.

Height: 2 to 2½'.

Soil: Well-drained, average.

Light: Full sun.

Moisture: Drought resistant.

Planting time: For early bloom, start indoors under lights 8 weeks before last frost, March 1 in most parts of the country, or sow outdoors in situ after all danger of frost.

Bloom time: Early summer to killing frost.

Length of bloom: 3 to 4 months.

Live arrangements: Yes.

Vase life: Indefinitely.

Drying: Yes. Hang dry.

Tips: Harvest flowers for drying in late summer or early fall.

Strawflower
(Helichrysum)

Plant type: Annual.

Color: Many varieties in a wide range of colors except blue and green.

Description: Daisy-shaped blossoms on medium green foliage.

Height: 1 to 2'.

Soil: Well-drained, average.

Light: Full sun.

Moisture: Drought resistant.

Planting time: For early bloom, start indoors under lights 8 weeks before last frost, March 1 in most parts of the country, or sow outdoors in situ after all danger of frost.

Planting instructions: Surface sow.

Bloom time: Early summer to killing frost.

Length of bloom: 3 to 4 months.

Live arrangements: Yes.

Vase life: 7 to 14 days.

Drying: Yes. Hang dry.

Tips: Harvest flowers for drying in late summer or early fall.

7

The Foolproof Cut-flower Garden: Bulbs

. . .

Certainly one of the most nearly foolproof cut-flower gardens you can install in your landscape is one made up of spring-blooming bulbs, both the "major" bulbs (daffodils, tulips, hyacinths, and Dutch crocuses) and the often overlooked "minor" bulbs—scilla, grape hyacinth, snowdrops, and the charming mini-daffodils, glory-of-the-snow, and others.

Virtually insect- and disease-free, all bulbs require is soil preparation at fall planting time and some annual feeding. And every year, from the first spring on, most bulbs reward you with a dazzling display of glorious color and armsful of cutting material for indoor arrangements.

WHERE TO BUY BULBS. Toward the end of summer and on into the fall, nurseries, garden centers, and many supermarkets sell bulbs; however, the selection may be limited. Many mail-order nurseries (see Sources) offer a very large selection. It is a good idea to write for catalogs by June. Study the catalogs, along with the individual bulb entries that follow, and then place your order by the end of July or early August. This way you will be assured of getting what you want, avoiding the disappointment of having varieties you want sold out. Most mail-order nurseries deliver bulbs at the proper planting time for your area.

WHERE TO PLANT BULBS. You can install a cut-flower bulb planting virtually anywhere on your property—

Early-blooming crocuses and snowdrops can be used in mini-arrangements to brighten the indoors during late winter and look lovely together outside in the garden as well.

Several years ago, Alfred Smith of Peconic, New York, went somewhat overboard and installed this enormous tulip planting. Surely it provides enough cutting material to fill several houses with lush spring bouquets.

in flower beds and borders, interplanted among foundation plantings, along driveways and walks, around mailboxes and birdbaths, naturalized in fields, under deciduous trees, or in woods. Use your imagination and plant them anywhere you want, but be aware of the following rules of bulb aesthetics:

- Plant at least twelve of the major bulbs together, preferably of one color. It is better to plant twenty-four if your budget permits. In this way, your planting makes a statement and you will have plenty of cutting material available for arrangements. "Minor" bulbs should be planted in groups of no less than fifty, preferably one hundred.
- Never buy a rainbow mixture of bulbs. The result at bloom time is a hodgepodge of color, ineffective and often messy-looking, and hardly appro-

priate for the indoor flower arrangements you will want to create.

- Avoid planting in a straight line or in a single circle around a tree or bush, for the results are feeble-looking.
- Consider the landscape not only from the outdoor point of view, but from indoors through your windows. Since bulbs begin blooming in late February and continue on through the spring, plan your outdoor plantings of early-blooming bulbs so that you can enjoy them from inside as well. Chances are with late winter and early spring cold and rain, you won't be spending too much time outdoors enjoying your garden, although installing early-blooming bulbs near the doorway is a good idea because you can enjoy their color as you come and go in and out of the house.
- For displays in distant parts of your property,

plant large groups of a single variety in drifts rather than in symmetrical beds. The effect is more natural-looking and, thus, more dramatic.

• Although not of an aesthetic nature, this tip will prove to be invaluable: Beware of bargains. Bulbs are quite inexpensive and bargain collections are usually of inferior quality. As a rule, with most planting stock you get what you pay for. There are, however, two exceptions to this rule. Many mail-order bulb suppliers offer mixtures of daffodils for naturalizing at reduced prices. These are certainly worth the money *if* you plan on using them to naturalize in meadows or under deciduous trees. The other exception is end-of-season sales at nurseries and garden centers. Individual varieties of bulbs are often reduced in price toward the middle of November. Since there is still time to plant, you might wish to consider buying some of these to fill in your landscape several years after your initial planting. But don't avail yourself of these bargains when installing your initial bed, as selection is usually quite limited and has been picked over by others earlier during the season.

Brilliant scarlet 'Emperor' tulips overplanted with deep blue scilla are not only pleasing in the landscape but in arrangements as well.

SELECTING A SITE. The first consideration is light. Most bulbs require either full sun or partial shade in order to perform well. Very few thrive in deep shade, so avoid areas under evergreen trees, foundation plantings with a northern exposure, and other areas with little sunlight. The next thing to consider is drainage. All bulbs need good drainage to grow properly, so when you select your site, be sure that this requirement is met. Beyond the obvious, that is, swampy soil or areas where water gathers and stands after rain, you can test a planting site for proper drainage. To do this, dig a hole to the depth at which the bulbs will be planted; eight to twelve inches is a good depth. Fill the hole with water and allow it to soak in. Repeat this two more times. After the third time, let the water sit for six

to eight hours. If it's still there, the drainage is not sufficient for bulb growing, and you should select another site.

PLANNING A BULB PLANTING. The rules for planning a bulb planting are pretty much the same as for annuals (see page 46).

Consult the bulb sequence table on page 60 to see if varieties you wish to plant bloom at the same time or in sequence. For example, you will see on the chart that grape hyacinths bloom at the same time as most daffodils. In the garden as well as in mini-arrangements, the deep blue of the grape hyacinths and the yellows of the daffodils are very beautiful in combination. However, note that pur-

Spring Bloom Sequence Chart

Below is a chart of the approximate blooming dates of various spring bulbs in the warmer areas of Zones 5 and 6, and the colder areas of Zone 7. If you live in Zone 4, add a week, in Zone 3, add two weeks. In Zone 8, subtract a week. Consider these dates approximate; however, they will help you in planning a sequence of bloom. There is no summer bloom sequence chart as too many factors (temerature, rain, care) can affect summer bloomers' actual flowering times.

BULB	BLOOM TIME
Iris danfordiae	March 1–20
Snowdrops *(Galanthus)*	March 1–20
Crocus (Dutch)	March 10–25
Iris reticulata	March 10–25
Squill, striped *(Puschkinia scilloides)*	March 25–April 10
Grape hyacinth *(Muscari)*	April 10–25
Daffodils and Narcissus	April 10–30
Dutch hyacinth	April 15–30
Tulip—Early	April 15–30
Tulip—Darwin Hybrid	April 25–May 10
Tulip—Double Peony	April 25–May 10
Tulip—Lily Flowering	April 25–May 10
Tulip—Mendel	April 25–May 10
Tulip—Triumph	April 25–May 10
Tulip—Cottage	May 5–20
Tulip—Darwin	May 5–20
Tulip—Parrot	May 5–20
Lily-of-the-valley *(Convallaria majalis)*	May 30–June 15

ple crocus bloom well in advance of daffodils, thus at bloom time you will not have that combination in view, nor will you be able to combine them in arrangements. Often in mail-order bulb catalogs you will see photographs of a wide variety of bulbs all in bloom at the same time. These photos are misleading because the growers force some later-blooming varieties to flower with earlier-blooming varieties. Regardless of the photographs you may see, a crocus does not bloom at the same time as a Darwin tulip, but six to eight weeks earlier.

PREPARING THE SOIL. Soil types vary from very sandy, light texture to very heavy, clay texture. This is not only from one part of the country to another, but even within the confines of one's own property. For this reason, when installing a bulb planting, it is best to fortify and prepare the soil.

First, excavate the bed to a depth of one foot. Then mix the excavated soil with about one half as much organic material such as sphagnum peat moss, available in garden centers or nurseries, and/or well-rotted manure or compost. Never use fresh manure as it can burn tender roots. Then replace the mixture into the excavated bed. Water thoroughly. It is best to do this several days in advance of your planting schedule.

PLANTING BULBS. When you go to the garden to plant bulbs, be sure to bring a ruler with you so that you can measure appropriate depth and spacing of bulbs. Be sure you have your design scheme with you. Aside from the bulbs, you will need fertilizer. For many years it was universally thought that all-purpose 5-10-5 fertilizer plus bone meal were the best food for bulbs. However, recent research conducted by the Dutch bulb industry has revealed that bone meal is a waste of time and money. Today a fertilizer with a 9-9-6 ratio of nitrogen, phosphorus, and potassium secures the best results. This is available at many nurseries and garden centers, as well as from mail-order supply houses and is called Holland Bulb Booster. As a general rule, before planting, dig a hole twice as deep as the recommended depth for a particular bulb. Mix the fertilizer with the soil at the rate of one tablespoon per square foot, three quarters cup per ten square feet, four cups per fifty square feet. Replace the soil to the recommended planting level. Next, flatten out the bottom of the planting hole by patting it gently with your hand. You do this to provide an even surface for the bulbs so they won't fall on their sides when you fill the hole in with soil. Set the bulbs in place, pointed end up, and gently press them into the soil. Cover the bulbs with the rest of the soil, tamp down lightly, then water thoroughly. If there are dry spells in your area during the fall, be sure to water the planting thoroughly at least once a week.

WINTER MULCHING. In most areas of the country, a winter mulch is not necessary for bulb plantings. However, in far northern climates, zones 2 and 3, it is a good idea to apply a six-inch layer of salt hay, available at garden centers and nurseries, over the planting after the first deep frost. Remove this mulch in late winter or early spring as the bulbs just begin to emerge from the ground.

MAINTENANCE. In late winter or early spring, when bulbs begin to emerge from the ground, apply a dusting of 9-9-6 fertilizer (Holland Bulb Booster) at the rates recommended above for planting. Sprinkle the fertilizer evenly on the soil surface of the planting.

After bloom, remove spent blossoms by cutting the stalks of tulips, daffodils, hyacinths, and *Scilla hispanica*. Do *not* cut off foliage, as the leaves contain substantial amounts of nutrients necessary for next year's bloom. Allow the foliage to wither and dry naturally, then you can remove it. If you find the foliage unsightly, you can either tie it up in bundles with string or rubber bands, or overplant annuals in the area to hide the foliage and provide more cutting material during the summer. Spring-blooming bulbs do not need watering during the summer as they are dormant.

PESTS AND DISEASES. Although spring-flowering bulbs are virtually insect- and disease-free, most are not animal- or rodent-proof. That is, except for all daffodils, narcissus, and most scilla. Their bulbs and foliage are poisonous to animals and rodents, so they do not nibble at them either above or below ground. However, all other spring-flowering bulbs are taste treats for deer, raccoons, rabbits, chipmunks, and burrowing creatures such as moles and voles.

If deer and raccoons find your available plantings a lovely snack, about the only thing you can do is to sprinkle dried blood meal on the shoots when they emerge. This is available at garden centers and nurseries and, in fact, also serves as fertilizer for emerging bulbs.

Rabbits and chipmunks find tulips and crocus delectable. I have found that dried blood meal does deter them; however, after rain, you must renew applications. Beyond this, I have found that placing a piece of one-inch mesh chicken wire over the entire planting helps to keep them away. Once the emerging shoots are several inches tall, the rodents don't seem to savor them. Then I remove the chicken wire.

Moles burrow beneath the ground and eat bulbs. They are attracted by grubs which live beneath the surface of lawns, eating the grass roots. If you can rid your lawn of grubs, the moles will probably go away and not bother your bulb plantings. Milky spore is a natural, nontoxic insecticide which is available at garden centers and nurseries which you can apply to your lawn to kill grubs. Check with your local cooperative extension, listed in the phone book under county government, for further information regarding what is recommended and/or permitted for use in your area.

Recently there have been plagues of vole infestations in various parts of the country. These rodents eat not only bulbs but the roots of fruit trees, azaleas, evergreens, etc. At present, there is little that can be done to rid your property of these creatures, except keeping one of their natural enemies, cats, in and around your garden.

Inquire locally at nurseries and garden centers, or from neighbors about the vole and mole problem and, if it is serious, run a trial planting of a few bulbs to see if the burrowing rodents are present and hungry before you install a large and expensive planting. I have tried many suggested ways to prevent moles and voles from eating tulips, crocus, and other bulbs, and found that the most effective way is to plant bulbs in large plastic or rubberized pots and then sink them into the ground with their rims at soil level. But sometimes even this doesn't work. Lining plantings with flexible gutter wire before setting out bulbs is another method I have used. Other than that, keep in mind that daffodils and scilla are impervious to animal and rodent damage and plant only those.

Spring-flowering Bulbs

Spring-flowering bulbs are planted the previous fall. If you order from a mail-order nursery, most ship at the proper planting time for your zone. If you purchase them at a nursery, inquire as to when to plant. In Zones 5 to 7, the best time to plant is from mid-October through late November. In Zone 8, you can plant into the beginning of December. In Zones 4 northward, early September through early October is a good time to plant.

Crocus, Dutch

USDA zones: 4 to 7.
Color: Purple, white, blue, gold, yellow, and combinations thereof.
Description: Chalice-shaped 1 to 2″ blossoms on handsome silver-and-green spearlike foliage.
Height: 4 to 6″.
Soil: Well-drained, ordinary soil fortified with sphagnum peat moss and well-rotted compost or manure.
Light: Full sun or partial shade.
Moisture: Water only if spring season is dry.
Planting time: Late September or early October; however, may be planted as long as soil is workable.
Planting instructions: Depth, 4″; distance apart, 4 to 6″.
Growing season care: Allow foliage to ripen and wither before removing it.
Bloom time: Early spring.
Length of bloom: 3 weeks.
Rodentproof: No.
Forcing: Yes. Use 9 cm. or larger size bulbs. Almost all cultivars can be used, but the Netherlands Flower Bulb Information Center recommends the following:

'Remembrance' (lavender)
'Flower Record' (lavender)
'Victor Hugo' (lavender)
'Pickwick' (striped lavender and silvery white)
'Joan of Arc' (white)
'Peter Pan' (white)
'Large Yellow' (yellow)

Live arrangements: Yes.
Vase life: 2 to 4 days.
Drying: No.
Propagation: Dig every 3 years after foliage has dried, separate bulb clumps, and replant as above.
Tips: Although they are suitable for forcing, because of their very short stems, crocus does not lend itself readily to cut-flower arrangements. However, if preconditioned and conditioned they can be used in miniature arrangements, often with great charm.

About a dozen different varieties of daffodils have been included in this stunning arrangement. Arrangement by Lucille Siracusano, Feather Hill Country Flowers and Gifts.

Daffodil

(Narcissus)

USDA zones: 3 to 9.

Color: White, yellow, gold, orange, apricot.

Description: There are 11 basic types of narcissus according to the system established by the Royal Horticultural Society of Great Britain and followed by bulb growers throughout the world. Shapes include the familiar trumpet, small-cupped, large-cupped, double, and so forth. All grow on erect stems over swordlike medium green foliage.

Height: 3″ to 2′.

Soil: Well-drained, ordinary soil fortified with sphagnum peat moss and well-rotted compost or manure.

Light: Full sun or partial shade.

Moisture: Water only if spring season is dry.

Planting time: October; however, may be planted as long as soil is workable. I have known people who forgot to plant, installed them in early spring, and they not only survived, but bloomed.

Planting instructions: Depth, three times the diameter of the bulb; distance apart, six to eight inches, depending on the size of the bulb.

Growing season care: Don't remove foliage until completely withered and brown. Each spring, when shoots emerge, scratch in 1 tablespoon of 9-9-6 fertilizer per square foot of planting area.

Bloom time: Early to midspring, depending on variety and location of planting.

Length of bloom: 2 to 3 weeks.

Rodentproof: Yes.

Forcing: Yes. Purchase DN I or DN II size bulbs. The Netherlands Flower Bulb Information Center recommends the following cultivars for forcing:

Large trumpets
'Dutch Master' (yellow)
'Explorer' (yellow)
'Golden Harvest' (yellow)
'Mt. Hood' (white)
'Unsurpassable' (yellow)

Narcissus (Large-Cupped)
'Carlton' (yellow)
'Flower Record' (white with orange cup)
'Ice Follies' (white)
'Yellow Sun' (yellow)

Narcissus (Small-Cupped)
'Barrett Browning' (white with orange cup)

Narcissus (Double)
'Bridal Crown' (white with orange center)

The Foolproof Cut-flower Garden: Bulbs

Live arrangements: Yes.

Vase life: 4 to 6 days.

Drying: Yes. Silica dry.

Propagation: When bloom begins to diminish, dig bulbs after foliage has dried, separate, and re-plant as above.

Tips: Daffodils are probably the most universally grown and loved of all the spring-flowering bulbs, for practical as well as aesthetic reasons, for they are not only pest- and disease-free, but rodent-proof as well. Most varieties perform well over a period of 5, 10, or even 15 to 20 years.

WARNING: *If you use daffodils for forcing, keep in mind that the bulbs are poisonous to dogs, cats, and human beings only if eaten, and can be fatal. Flowers and foliage are not poisonous.*

Daffodil, Miniature

USDA zones: 3 to 9.

Color: Yellow, orange, or white, and combinations thereof.

Description: Trumpet or double blossoms held on stalks over medium green, spearlike foliage.

Height: 6 to 14″.

Soil: Well-drained, ordinary soil fortified with sphagnum peat moss and well-rotted compost or manure.

Light: Full sun or partial shade.

Moisture: Water only if spring season is dry.

Planting time: October; however, may be planted as long as soil is workable.

Planting instructions: Depth, 3 to 5″; distance apart, 4 to 6″.

Growing season care: Don't remove foliage until completely withered and brown. Each spring, when shoots emerge, scratch in 1 tablespoon of 9-9-6 fertilizer per square foot of planting area.

Bloom time: Early to midspring.

Length of bloom: 3 weeks.

Rodentproof: Yes.

Forcing: Yes. Use DN I or DN II size bulbs. The Netherlands Flower Bulb Information Center recommends the following cultivars:

'February Gold' (yellow)
'Jack Snipe' (white with yellow trumpet)
'Peeping Tom' (yellow)
'Tete-a-Tete' (yellow)

Live arrangements: Yes.

Vase life: 4 to 6 days.

Drying: Yes. Silica dry.

Propagation: When bloom begins to diminish, dig bulbs after foliage has dried, separate, and re-plant as above.

Tips: These mini-size versions of the standard daffodils add great charm to the landscape and are very useful in early spring miniature arrangements. Still, many gardeners have not yet discovered them. They are very reasonable in price. Those listed in the chart to the right are recommended for cutting.

WARNING: *If you use daffodils for forcing, keep in mind that the bulbs are poisonous to dogs, cats, and human beings only if eaten, and can be fatal. Flowers and foliage are not poisonous.*

Hyacinth, Dutch
(Hyacinthus orientalis)

USDA zones: 4 to 9.

Color: Blue, purple, red, pink, yellow, cream, white, orange-peach.

Description: Columnar spikes of florets held over jade green, straplike foliage.

Height: 8 to 12″.

Soil: Well-drained, ordinary soil fortified with sphagnum peat moss and well-rotted compost or manure.

CULTIVAR	COLOR	HEIGHT (INCHES)
'April Tears'	Deep yellow	6–8
'Baby Moon'	Buttercup yellow	9
'Double Jonquil'	Double, bright yellow	10
'February Gold'	Bright yellow and lemon	8
'Gold Drops'	Yellow and white	10
'Hawera'	Creamy yellow	8
'Hoop Petticoat'	Bright yellow	6
'Jack Snipe'	White and yellow	8
'Liberty Bells'	Clusters of yellow	8
'Lintie'	Yellow with orange rim	9
'Little Witch'	Deep yellow	6
'Peeping Tom'	Golden yellow	8
'Pipit'	Sulfur and white	9
'Rip Van Winkle'	Double, clear yellow	6
'Suzy'	Yellow and orange	14
'Tete-a-Tete'	Yellow	8

Light: Full sun or partial shade.

Moisture: Water only if spring season is dry.

Planting time: Late September or early October; however, may be planted as long as soil is workable.

Planting instructions: Depth, 5 to 6″; distance apart, 5″.

Growing season care: Don't remove foliage until completely withered and brown. Each spring, when shoots emerge, scratch in 1 tablespoon of 9-9-6 fertilizer per square foot of planting area.

Bloom time: Early to midspring.

Length of bloom: 3 weeks.

Rodentproof: Yes.

Forcing: Yes. Use $^{17}/_{18}$ cm. and $^{18}/_{19}$ cm. bulbs for earliest forcing or purchase "prepared" bulbs. They are the easiest to force. The Netherlands Flower Bulb Information Center recommends the following cultivars for forcing:

'Delft Blue' (blue)

'Ostara' (blue)

A single hyacinth arranged with foliage will scent an entire room.

The Foolproof Cut-flower Garden: Bulbs

'Carnegie' (white)
'L'Innocence' (white)
'Amsterdam' (red)
'Anna Marie' (pink)
'Pink Pearl' (pink)

Live arrangements: Yes.
Vase life: 2 to 6 days.
Drying: No.
Propagation: It is best to purchase new bulbs rather than to try to propagate from existing stock.
Tips: Familiar to all, hyacinths are easily grown in the garden; however, their stiff appearance makes them difficult to use effectively in most floral arrangements. But, after the first year of bloom, the stalks of florets loosen up substantially, taking on a lovely, informal look and are interesting in spring bouquets. They bear a lovely scent in both the garden and as cut flowers indoors.
WARNING: *If you use hyacinth for indoor arrangements, keep in mind that the bulbs are poisonous to dogs, cats, and human beings only if eaten, and can be fatal. Flowers and foliage are not poisonous.*

Hyacinth, Grape
(Muscari)

USDA zones: 5 to 7 or 8.
Color: Bright blue, pale blue, or white, depending on variety.
Description: Clusters of florets resembling upside-down bunches of grapes held on stems over sprawling, straplike foliage.
Height: 4 to 12″.
Soil: Well-drained, ordinary soil fortified with sphagnum peat moss and well-rotted compost or manure.
Light: Full sun or partial shade.
Moisture: Water only if spring season is dry.

Planting time: October; however, may be planted as long as soil is workable.
Planting instructions: Depth, 3″; distance apart, 3″.
Growing season care: Allow foliage to ripen and wither before removing it. No need to fertilize after the original planting.
Bloom time: Midspring.
Length of bloom: 3 weeks.
Rodentproof: No.
Forcing: Yes. *Muscari armeniacum* is recommended. Use 9 or 10 cm. bulbs.
Live arrangements: Yes.
Vase life: 7 to 14 days.
Drying: No.
Propagation: It is best to leave bulbs undisturbed; since they are so inexpensive, it is hardly worth dividing them. However, if you do decide to, dig them up after bloom, remove the small bulbs that have developed around the larger ones, and replant.
Tips: Varieties recommended for cutting are *M. armeniacum* (common grape hyacinth), *M.a. album* (white), *M.a.* 'Blue Spike', and *M. plumosum* (feather hyacinth). All perfume the surrounding air with a lovely, subtle sweet fragrance.

Iris danfordiae

USDA zones: 3 to 8.
Color: Yellow.
Description: Blossoms with irislike standards and falls, held on stems over grasslike foliage.
Height: 6″.
Soil: Ordinary, with good drainage.
Light: Full sun or partial shade.
Moisture: Water only if spring season is dry.
Planting time: October; however, may be planted as long as soil is workable.
Planting instructions: Depth, 3 to 4″; distance apart, 3 to 4″.

Growing season care: Don't remove foliage until completely withered and brown. Each spring, when shoots emerge, scratch in 1 tablespoon of 9-9-6 fertilizer per square foot of planting area.

Bloom time: Late winter or early spring.

Length of bloom: 1 to 2 weeks.

Rodentproof: Yes.

Forcing: Yes. The Netherlands Flower Bulb Information Center recommends that you use 6 cm. bulbs or larger.

Live arrangements: Yes.

Vase life: 4 to 6 days.

Drying: No.

Propagation: Bulbs rarely multiply. Purchase new bulbs if more stock is desired.

Tips: Although they rarely bloom a second year, these charming bright yellow blossoms are worth the effort of planting every fall, just to provide sparkling yellow color to the late winter landscape.

Iris reticulata

USDA zones: 3 to 8.

Color: Light blue, lavender, and purple, depending on variety.

Description: Iris-shaped blossoms held on stems over grasslike foliage.

Height: 6″.

Soil: Ordinary, with good drainage.

Light: Full sun or partial shade.

Moisture: Water only if spring season is dry.

Planting time: October; however, may be planted as long as soil is workable.

Planting instructions: Depth, 3 to 4″; distance apart, 3 to 4″.

Growing season care: Don't remove foliage until completely withered and brown. Each spring, when shoots emerge, scratch in 1 tablespoon of 9-9-6 fertilizer per square foot of planting area.

Bloom time: Late winter or early spring.

Length of bloom: 1 to 2 weeks.

Rodentproof: Yes.

Forcing: Yes. All varieties are suitable but 'Harmony' is best. Use 6 cm. bulbs or larger.

Live arrangements: Yes.

Vase life: 4 to 6 days.

Drying: No.

Propagation: Difficult. Purchase new bulbs at fall planting time if you want more.

Tips: Among the earliest of spring-blooming bulbs, their lovely violetlike fragrance is irresistible in miniature arrangements.

Lily-of-the-Valley
(Convallaria majelis)

USDA zones: 2 to 7. Not suitable for warmer climates.

Color: White or pink.

Description: Bell-shaped blossoms with a lovely fragrance held on stems over broad, medium green foliage.

Height: 8″.

Soil: Slightly acid; add sphagnum peat moss and a handful of Miracid to the planting site.

Light: Partial shade.

Moisture: Moist conditions.

Planting time: October; however, may be planted as long as soil is workable.

Planting instructions: Depth, 1″; distance apart, 3 to 4″.

Growing season care: Don't remove foliage until completely withered and brown. Mulch each fall with compost or sphagnum peat moss.

Bloom time: Late spring.

Length of bloom: 2 weeks.

Rodentproof: Yes.

Forcing: Yes, but use only prechilled, potted rhizomes available at garden centers, nurseries, or through some mail-order sources.

Live arrangements: Yes.

Vase life: 3 to 6 days.

Drying: No.

Propagation: Divide and replant pips in fall when foliage starts to yellow.

Tips: These old-fashioned favorites are very easily grown and, beyond their charm in small bouquets, their foliage serves as an excellent non-invasive ground cover in shady areas.

WARNING: *If you use this for indoor arrangements, keep in mind that the leaves and flowers are poisonous to dogs, cats, and human beings if eaten, and although death will not result, high temperatures, digestive upset, and mental confusion will.*

Snowdrop
(Galanthus)

USDA zones: 2 to 9.

Color: Translucent white.

Description: Bell-shaped ½" blossoms held on stalks over slender, medium green foliage.

Height: 3 to 8".

Soil: Well-drained, ordinary soil fortified with sphagnum peat moss and well-rotted compost or manure.

Light: Full sun or partial shade.

Moisture: Water only if spring season is dry.

Planting time: Late September and early October; however, may be planted as long as soil is workable.

Planting instructions: Depth, 2 to 4"; distance apart, 2 to 3".

Growing season care: Don't remove foliage until completely withered and brown. No need to fertilize after the original planting.

Bloom time: Late winter to early spring.

Length of bloom: 3 to 4 weeks.

Rodentproof: Yes.

Forcing: No.

Live arrangements: Yes.

Vase life: 3 to 6 days.

Drying: No.

Propagation: It is best to leave bulbs undisturbed; they are so inexpensive, it is hardly worth dividing them. However, if you decide to, dig them up after they bloom, remove the small bulbs that have developed around the larger ones, and replant.

Tips: Charming in miniature arrangements. Will self-sow in the landscape and naturalize if conditions are favorable. Regarded an endangered species, *G. nivalis* (common snowdrop) is not harvested in the wild. All others are, so do not purchase unless label states "Bulbs Grown from Cultivated Stock."

Squill, Striped
(Puschkinia scilloides)

USDA zones: 2 to 9.

Color: Bluish white or white.

Description: Clusters of ½ to 1" blossoms held on stalks over straplike leaves.

Height: 4 to 8".

Soil: Well-drained, ordinary. Do not enrich the soil or add fertilizer.

Light: Full sun or partial shade.

Moisture: Water only if spring season is dry.

Planting time: October; however, may be planted as long as soil is workable.

Planting instructions: Depth, 2 to 3"; distance apart, 2 to 3".

Growing season care: If you don't want puschkinia to throw seedlings, remove its blossoms when spent. Allow the foliage to ripen and wither before removing it.

Bloom time: Early spring.

Length of bloom: 3 to 4 weeks.

Rodentproof: No.

Pale blue squill is another natural for early spring mini-arrangements.

Forcing: No.

Live arrangements: Yes.

Vase life: 3 to 6 days.

Drying: No.

Propagation: It is best to leave bulbs undisturbed; they are so inexpensive, it is hardly worth dividing them. However, if you decide to, dig them up after they bloom, remove the small bulbs that have developed around the larger ones, and replant.

Tips: Charming in miniature arrangements. Will self-sow in the landscape and naturalize if conditions are favorable.

Tulip, Dutch

USDA zones: 3 to 7.

Color: Every color except blue.

Description: Single and double turban-shaped flowers held on erect stems over medium green, broad-leaved foliage, depending on variety.

Height: 18 to 36″.

Soil: Well-drained, ordinary soil fortified with sphagnum peat moss and well-rotted compost or manure.

Light: Full sun or partial shade.

Moisture: Water only if spring season is dry.

Planting time: November; however, may be planted as long as soil is workable. In northern areas plant in October before ground freezes.

Planting instructions: Depth, 6 to 8″; distance apart, 6″.

Growing season care: Don't remove foliage until completely withered and brown. Each spring, when shoots emerge, scratch in 1 tablespoon of 9-9-6 fertilizer per square foot of planting area.

Bloom time: Early to late spring, depending on variety.

Length of bloom: 2 to 3 weeks, depending on variety.

Rodentproof: No. Very susceptible to rodents who relish not only the foliage above ground, but the bulbs below.

Forcing: Yes. Use 12 cm. and up bulbs. The Netherlands Flower Bulb Information Center recommends the following cultivars:

Red: 'Bing Crosby', 'Capri', 'Cassini', 'Charles', 'Paul Richter', 'Prominence', 'Ruby Red', 'Trance

Pink or rose: 'Blenda', 'Cantor', 'Christmas Marvel', 'Gander', 'Preludium'

A drift of 'Apricot Beauty' tulips provide ample cutting material for spring arrangements.

Yellow: 'Bellona', 'Golden Melody', 'Kareol', 'Monte Carlo'

White: 'Hibernia', 'Pax', 'Snowstar'

Lavender: 'Attila', 'Prince Charles'

Orange: 'Orange Monarch'

Apricot: 'Apricot Beauty'

Bicolored red and white: 'Leen Van Der Mark', 'Lucky Strike', 'Merry Widow', 'Mirjoran'

Bicolored red and yellow: 'Abra', 'Golden Mirjoran', 'Kees Nelis', 'Thule'

Live arrangements: Yes.
Vase life: 6 to 8 days.
Drying: No.
Propagation: This can be done only by experts.
Tips: If you select from early, midseason, and late season varieties, you can extend the tulip cutting season to two months.

Summer-blooming Bulbs

The following bulbs must be planted in the spring, after all danger of frost has passed, rather than in the fall. Check the sources list and write for catalogs in February or March.

Crocosmia or Montbretia

USDA zones: Hardy in Zones 8 to 11; in Zones 7 and north, dig up bulbs after frost and store as directed below.
Color: Yellow, orange, scarlet.
Description: 1 ½" blooms held on stalks with spear-like medium green foliage.
Height: 2 to 4".
Soil: Ordinary.
Light: Full sun.
Moisture: Water during prolonged summer drought.
Planting time: Spring, after all danger of frost.
Planting instructions: Depth, 2"; distance apart, 3".
Growing season care: Scratch a light dusting of 5-10-5 fertilizer into the soil when plants emerge, and 3 to 4 weeks later. Stake plants when 1' high.
Bloom time: Late summer and early fall.
Length of bloom: 2 to 4 weeks.
Rodentproof: Yes.
Forcing: No.
Winter care: In Zones 8 to 11, winter over in ground. In Zones 7 and north, dig up the bulbs

A very trendy blossom used in contemporary arrangements is this brilliant scarlet Crocosmia *'Lucifer'.*

These mignonette dahlias offer profuse bloom all summer and well into the fall.

after frost nips the tops of the plants. Leave the soil on the corms and dry for several days in an airy, shady, frost-free place. Store with the soil on the corms in dry sphagnum peat moss, perlite, or vermiculite at 50° to 55°F.

Tips: 'Lucifer' is a brilliant red variety that adds a jewellike quality to an arrangement.

Dahlia

USDA zones: Although hardy in Zones 10 and 11, it is preferable to dig the bulbs up after the bloom season. In Zones 9 and north, dig up in fall and store as directed below.

Color: Every color except blue and true green. Many multicolors.

Description: Blossoms range from less than 1″ to over 1′ in diameter, held on stiff, erect stems over lush, dark green, serrated foliage. The taller-growing varieties which produce immense flowers are inappropriate for arrangements.

Height: 1 to 7′.

Soil: Well-drained, liberally enriched with sphagnum peat moss and compost or rotted cow manure.

Light: Full sun, but will grow in partial shade, although not as strongly.

Moisture: Keep well-watered. Mulch to conserve moisture.

Planting time: Spring, after all danger of frost.

Planting instructions: Dig a hole 6 by 6″ and work a cup of 5-10-5 fertilizer into the bottom of it. Set one root in the bottom with the stem end facing up, spreading the attached tubers like the hands of a clock in the hole. Cover with 2″ of soil and water thoroughly.

As the shoots grow, gradually fill in the hole with soil. Once the hole has been filled in and the plants are 3″ tall, thin out all but four or five shoots. When these shoots have two pairs of leaves, pinch out the growing tip just above the upper set of leaves to encourage bushy growth. It is not necessary to pinch shorter varieties a second time. Space the planting holes 1′ apart.

Growing season care: Scratch a light dusting of 5-10-5 fertilizer into the soil when the plants are well established, and water in thoroughly. Staking is unnecessary with shorter varieties.

Bloom time: Midsummer to frost.

Length of bloom: 2 to 4 weeks.

Rodentproof: Yes.

Forcing: No.

Live arrangements: Yes.

Vase life: 5 to 7 days.

Drying: No.

Winter care: When the stalks have yellowed or been nipped by frost, dig a 2′-diameter circle around the plant and gently pry it up with a pitchfork. Shake off the loose soil, being careful not to break the roots, and let the clump dry in the sun for several hours. Gently remove any remaining soil. Place in single layer in a plastic-lined box and cover with dry sand, peat moss, vermiculite, perlite, or sawdust. Store in a dark, dry, cool place (40° to 45°F) until spring. Check occasionally during the winter for signs of shriveling, lightly moistening the storage material if necessary.

Spring propagation: Divide the clumps with a sharp knife, making sure that each separate root is attached to a portion of stalk with a visible growth eye. Do this in spring, two to four weeks before outdoor planting time. (Place these divided roots in moist sand to plump them up and encourage sprouting after dividing and before planting.)

Gladiolus

USDA zones: Hardy in Zones 8 to 11, but for best blooming results, dig up in fall. For Zone 7 and north, dig up the bulbs in the fall and store as directed below.

Color: All colors of the rainbow.

Description: Columns of blossoms held on stalks with medium green spearlike foliage.

Height: 1 to 5′.

Soil: Light, sandy loam, but will grow in ordinary soil enriched with sphagnum peat moss and compost. Avoid using manures, as they can cause bulb rot.

Light: Full sun.

Moisture: Water regularly during prolonged summer drought.

Planting time: Spring, after all danger of frost.

Planting instructions: Depth, 4 to 6″; distance apart, 4 to 6″.

Growing season care: Scratch a light dusting of 5-10-5 fertilizer into the soil when plants emerge and 3 to 4 weeks later. Stake plants when 1′ high.

Bloom time: Throughout summer and fall, depending on planting date.

Length of bloom: 2 weeks.

Rodentproof: Yes.

Forcing: No.

Live arrangements: Yes.

Vase life: 7 to 14 days.

Drying: No.

Propagation: Although the small corms which form around the mother corm can be separated and planted, it takes several years of planting, digging in the fall, and replanting for them to grow to flowering size. It is best to buy new corms at spring planting time if you want more stock.

Winter care: Dig the bulbs up after bloom in Zones 10 and 11 or when the frost nips the tops of the plants in all other zones. Leave the soil on the corms and dry for several days in an airy, shady, frost-free place. Store with the soil on the corms in dry sphagnum peat moss, perlite, or vermiculite at 50° to 55°F.

Tips: Gladiolus are best grown in the cutting garden and can be used to add dramatic vertical touches to indoor flower arrangements. Be sure to snip off unopened buds at the very top of the spike, for they will not open once cut.

Lily
(Lilium)

USDA zones: 3 to 11.

Color: All colors except blue.

Description: Depending on variety, 4 to 8″ star- and trumpet-shaped blossoms held on stalks with glossy, dark green leaves.

Height: 2 to 8′.

Soil: Ordinary soil enriched with sphagnum peat moss and compost or well-rotted manure.

Light: Full sun to partial shade.

Moisture: Water well during prolonged summer drought.

Planting time: Spring is best, but you can also plant in summer or fall.

Planting instructions: Dig a hole 1′ across and 1′ deep and mix a handful of all-purpose 5-10-5 fertilizer in the bottom of the hole. It is a good idea to mix about one tablespoon of an acid-type fertilizer such as Miracid into the hole as well. Mix fertilizer at bottom of hole with enough soil so that hole is 6 to 8 inches deep. Plant the bulbs, tamp down the soil, and water thoroughly. After planting, mulch heavily as lilies thrive in cool, moist soil.

Distance apart: Small bulbs: 6″; large bulbs (those the size of a fist): 18″.

Growing season care: Since only shorter varieties of lilies are recommended for arrangements,

Rubrum lillies are one of the most popular flowers of all for midsummer arrangements.

staking should not be necessary. After bloom, deadhead. In fall, after the killing frost, remove the withered stalks. If you cut lilies for bouquets, do not cut them with long stems, as food for next year's bloom is contained in the stems and leaves. Renew the mulch each year to ensure cool growing conditions for the roots. Each spring, scratch in a handful of acid-type fertilizer around the base of each plant.

Bloom time: Mid- to late summer, depending on variety.

Length of bloom: 2 to 4 weeks, depending on variety.

Rodentproof: Yes.

VARIETY	HEIGHT	DESCRIPTION
Album	3–4'	Pure white, new and expensive, but a showstopper
Auratum	3–4'	Large, pure white with golden bands and dark red spots; petal edges are ruffled, very fragrant.
'Bi-Centennial'	3–4'	Glowing rose with white edges
'Stargazer'	18"	Deep pink with dark red spots and bright white petal edges; a dwarf variety
'Uchida'	4–5'	The best known of the speciosums, with graceful, large flowers of rich pink shading to brilliant crimson at the center of the petal, with dark red spots all over.

Forcing: Yes, but best left to professionals.

Live arrangements: Yes.

Vase life: 6 to 8 days.

Drying: No.

Propagation: When planting becomes very crowded, in anywhere from three to ten years, dig after foliage has yellowed, separate bulb clumps, and replant individual bulbs.

Tips: When cutting lilies for bouquets, it is best to remove the stamens from the bloom, for the pollen on them can stain fabric. Simply cut the stamens with scissors or pinch them out with your fingers. Try to be careful not to let any pollen fall on the flower petals, as it detracts from the beauty of the bloom.

Lilies are among the few summer-flowering bulbs which are hardy. They are highly fragrant, emitting a sweet scent which can sometimes be overpowering. A vast array is available, so you must be careful to select those that will work best for the arrangements you wish to create.

Blooming Bulbs for Winter

There are several kinds of bulbs which do not require forcing to bloom in winter. These, like the amaryllis and cyclamen, are all easily grown and offer glorious blossoms during the cold weather doldrums. These can usually be purchased locally toward the end of fall, in time for Christmas flowering, though many mail-order houses specializing in bulbs also offer them. Cyclamen are available at florists as plants, usually already in bloom.

SELECTING CONTAINERS. There are any number of containers which are appropriate for growing flowering bulbs. All require pots with drainage holes in the bottom. If you decide on a new or used clay or terra-cotta container, it must be treated before planting, as must used plastic containers.

Brand new terra-cotta or clay container. Soak overnight in water. This is done so that the container will not absorb water from the planting medium.

Used terra-cotta, clay, or plastic container. Soak overnight in a solution of 1 part household bleach to 3 parts water. This is done to kill any disease organisms which might be on the surface of the container.

PESTS AND DISEASES. Since almost all flowering bulb plants are resistant to pests and are practically disease-free, it is very unlikely that you will have to cope with these problems. However, since winter-blooming bulb plants are treated as houseplants, if you already have a collection of these, pests which might have taken hold on your existing collection may attack them. Here are the ones to watch for:

Aphids. Small gray or green insects which cling to the underside of leaves and to the stems. They feed on plant juices, causing the leaves to yellow, and spread very fast.

Remedy: Rinse foliage in soapy water or spray with an insecticide containing pyrethrum or rotenone.

Mealybugs. These hide under the leaves and resemble bits of cotton. They suck the juices from the plant and cause the foliage to turn pale or drop from the plant. Stunted growth will also result.

Remedy: Dip a cotton swab in alcohol and remove the bugs. Then wash the plant foliage with soapy water.

Mites. These are infinitesimal in size and cannot be seen with the naked eye. Effects are curling leaves, withered buds or leaf tips, and webs on the underside of leaves.

Remedy: Cut away and dispose of infected foliage. Spray with dicofol. However, if cyclamen mites attack your florist cyclamen plants, the only thing to do is throw them out.

Red spider. Its many cobwebs make the foliage look dusty. Leaves will turn yellow and drop.

Remedy: Dip the plant in a solution of two teaspoons malathion to one gallon of water.

Thrips. Tiny insects that leave a white mottled look on leaves.

Remedy: Spray with malathion according to manufacturer's instructions on label.

Whiteflies. If plant is disturbed, adult whiteflies rise like a cloud from it. Leaves turn pale or yellow and eventually drop.

Remedy: These are difficult to control. Spray with rotenone or malathion according to manufacturer's instructions on label once a week for one month.

INCREASING HUMIDITY. Some winter-blooming bulb plants require a high level of humidity. During the winter heating season, almost all homes suffer from very dry air conditions. There are many ways of raising the humidity level around your plants. Here are some of them:

- *Grouping*. The moisture evaporating from a group of plants will raise the humidity level and create a miniature microclimate.
- *Trays and pebbles*. Place plants on trays or deep saucers filled with pebbles or stones. Pour water into the tray to the level of the stones. Set plants on top of the stones but above the water level.
- *Radiators*. Place trays of water on nearby radiators.
- *Glass and marbles*. Put colorful marbles in glass containers and fill them with water. This not only raises humidity, but looks very attractive as well.
- *Colored bottles*. Fill a collection of colored bottles with water and intersperse them among plants.
- *Misting*. Purchase inexpensive misters at garden centers or nurseries and spray foliage daily.
- *Washing foliage*. This method not only serves to raise humidity, but to keep the plant clean, thus reducing pest and disease infestation. Use clean, lukewarm water and wash gently with a soft sponge.
- *Humidifier*. Probably the most effective way to raise humidity in a dry winter house, and, not only is this good for a plant, it is good for you as well.

Amaryllis
(Hippeastrum)

These spectacular flowering bulbs are among the easiest to bring to bloom, and each year more and more lovely varieties are offered at garden centers, nurseries, and in mail-order catalogs. They are rapidly becoming a classic Christmas plant, with their varying shades of red, pink, and white, complementing the holiday decor. Recently, dwarf versions have been introduced,

This startling amaryllis will brighten any interior during the winter holidays.

although as of now they are only available in scarlet. They are so popular, though, that other varieties will soon be available.

USDA zones: Hardy only in Zones 9 to 11. In all other zones, treat as houseplants.

Color: Red, pink, white, orange, scarlet, striped, and combinations thereof.

Description: Three or four 8- to 10″ lily-shaped blossoms held on erect stalks over medium green, straplike foliage.

Height: 1 to 2′.

Soil: To make two quarts of soil medium, enough to pot one bulb in an 8″ pot, mix together ⅔ quart peat moss, ⅔ quart packaged potting soil, and ⅔ quart sharp sand or perlite. Add ½ teaspoon of ground limestone.

Light: Southern exposure; plant requires at least 4 hours of direct sun a day.

Moisture: Once the stalk appears, keep plant moderately moist until leaves begin to yellow in late summer. It is a good idea to water very well when necessary and then wait to water again until the soil at the top of the pot is dusty and dry. At the end of the summer reduce the water, then withhold it completely during the rest period. Do this until about one month before you wish to start the plant growing again.

Humidity: Normal winter indoor humidity is sufficient.

Temperature: Moderate. Prefers 60° to 65°F at night and 70°F or higher in the daytime during the winter heating season.

Planting instructions:

1. Since amaryllis prefer moderately pot-bound growing conditions, select a container 4″ larger in diameter than the bulb; generally you can plant one bulb in an 8″ pot or three bulbs in a 12″ pot.

2. Place 1″ of drainage material in the bottom of the container. Fill the bottom few inches of the pot with planting medium (see above). Set the bulb on the planting medium so that fully one half of the bulb will be above the soil line. Adjust the bottom level of planting medium if necessary.

3. Fill the rest of the pot with planting medium to within one inch of top of pot. This is to facilitate watering.

4. Water thoroughly. Do not water again until the stalk appears. Place in a sunny window.

Fertilizing: Feed monthly from the time the stalk emerges to the dormant period with any liquid houseplant fertilizer, at half the recommended strength. Withhold fertilizer during the dormant period.
Time to plant: For Christmas bloom, start in October.
Growing season care: Remove faded flower petals. When last blossom has faded, cut the stalk about five inches above the point where it emerges from the bulb.
Postbloom care: After the bulb has bloomed, usually about two months after planting, it is exhausted. It is smaller, slightly soft, and must be rebuilt to bloom the following year. Allow the leaves to grow for at least six months. It is best to leave the bulb in the pot and care for it, rather than removing it and planting it in the garden. You can sink the pot into the ground in the garden if you wish. During this rebuilding period, the bulb should produce seven to eleven leaves. At the end of August, slowly withdraw water until the leaves wilt. This takes about three weeks. When yellow, cut the leaves off three inches above the neck. Rest the bulb for at least one month in a cool (45° to 55°F) dark place in its pot. Before restarting bulbs to growth, hose away some of the surface planting medium, without exposing the roots, and replace with fresh planting medium. Then move to a warm position (70°F) for three weeks. Do not water during this time. After this, you can start the bulb growing again.
Bloom time: About six weeks after the bulb comes out of dormancy.
Length of bloom: 2 to 3 weeks.
Live arrangements: Yes. Flowers can be cut and used in live arrangements with other material.
Vase life: 5 to 7 days.
Drying: No.
Propagation: After three or four years, it will be time to repot. Unpot the plant when its foliage has dried, remove the offsets, and store until ready to plant in a shady, dry, warm place. Offsets may flower the second year.

Cyclamen

Hybridizers have been busy creating a new generation of cyclamen, including many dwarf varieties that are compact and manageable as houseplants and come in a wide range of colors. Because of the very specific growing conditions it requires, it is best to purchase plants at your local florist, garden center, or nursery. However, once the plant has bloomed, it is easily brought back to bloom year in and year out.
USDA zones: Hardy only in Zones 10 and 11. In all other zones, treat as a houseplant.

Color: Pink, white, red, purple, and combinations thereof.

Description: Butterfly-shaped, 2 to 3″ blossoms held on stalks over lush, attractive, variegated foliage.

Height: 12 to 18″.

Soil: To make two quarts of soil medium, enough to pot one tuber in an 8″ pot, mix together ⅔ quart peat moss, ⅔ quart packaged potting soil, and ⅔ quart sharp sand or perlite. Add ½ teaspoon of ground limestone.

Light: Bright, indirect, or curtain-filtered sunlight.

Moisture: Water at least once a week, keeping evenly moist. Do not overwater.

Humidity: Mist daily and increase humidity in one of the ways described on page 75.

Temperature: Cool. Prefers 40° to 55°F at night and 65°F or lower during the daytime.

Growing instructions:

1. Purchase a plant in the fall and grow as instructed below.

2. In the spring, after the blooming cycle, remove the plant from the pot and plant outdoors in the garden. Water regularly during the summer and fertilize as directed below.

3. In the fall, before the first frost, dig the plant from garden and repot, using an 8″ pot. Place 1 inch of drainage material in bottom of container, and fill about one third of the pot with the planting medium. Set one tuber on the medium so that one third of the tuber will be above the soil line. Adjust the bottom level of the planting medium if necessary. Fill the rest of the pot with planting medium to within 1 inch of the top of the pot. This is to facilitate watering. Water thoroughly.

Fertilizing: During the indoor growing season, feed once a week with any liquid houseplant

Florist cyclamen can be planted outdoors in spring and brought to bloom again indoors the following winter.

fertilizer at one third the recommended strength. During the outdoor growing season feed once a month at one third the recommended strength.

Growing season care: Remove spent flowers and foliage.

Bloom time: Fall and winter.

Length of bloom: Continuous throughout fall and winter.

Special instructions for Zones 10 and 11: Purchase plants in the fall for winter and spring bloom. Set plants 12 to 18″ apart with tubers half above the soil level. Discard after blooming.

8

The Permanent Cut-flower Collection

. . .

Perennials

Perennial flowering plants are the backbone of a cut-flower garden. They are permanent and winter hardy, that is, each fall when they have finished blooming, they die down, only to grow again the following spring. You do not have to plant them each spring as you do annuals. For this reason it is wise to plan carefully when installing a perennial cutting garden.

Included in the perennial cut-flower individual entries that follow are those genuses that are relatively nonproblematical, readily available, and to a great extent pest- and disease-free.

WHERE TO BUY PERENNIALS. With a few exceptions, most perennials are difficult to grow from seed. Often very special conditions must be provided, best left to experienced gardeners or professionals. This means that you ought to buy established plants in order to install a planting for your cut-flower garden.

In spring, most nurseries and garden centers offer perennial plants, usually in containers; however, unless the nursery specializes to a certain extent in these plants the selection will be limited. Beyond the nurseries and garden centers in your area, it is best to tap the vast resources of the mail-order garden supply houses, for the range of available varieties is almost unlimited. And usually the plant material is less expensive than that sold in the garden centers and nurseries. To best avail yourself of a wide selection, send away for catalogs, then look through them for flowers included in the perennial entries. Check the

Perennial gayfeather, purple coneflower, and yarrow can all be used in summer arrangements.

photographs of those plants not illustrated in the individual entries to see if they are suitable for your cut-flower needs. Then make your selection and send in your order. It is best to do this in January or February to be sure that the plants you want will not be sold out.

Beyond purchasing plants, friends, family, and neighbors can be an excellent source for stock, as most experienced gardeners know that to maintain vigor, perennials must be divided regularly and replanted.

PLANTING PERENNIALS. Perennials can be planted in many different areas of your garden. They can be planted in herbaceous borders or island beds, or be used to brighten the landscape after spring-blooming bulbs have finished, to add dashes of color to monotonous foundation plantings, to dress up driveways and walks, to enhance areas around birdbaths, garden furniture, and mailboxes, or to add color to shaded woodland areas. There are perennials suitable for just about every conceivable growing condition. Here are a few tips on how to use perennials in the landscape:

- With the possible exception of peonies, one single plant of which is substantial enough to make a statement, always plant at least three of each kind of plant. If you plant only one, the effect will be hodgepodge and spotty.
- Perennials are best used in an informal rather than formal manner. Most perennial plants are loose in structure, grow to varying heights, and look

Siberian iris adds a stately touch to an arrangement. Do not remove the pods after bloom because they can be used in fall and dried winter arrangements.

Hosta is so easy to grow and its foliage—variegated or solid—adds dramatic touches to any arrangement.

good when planted in groups next to other varieties, creating contrasts of texture, leaf color, flower color, and height. Stiff, geometrically planned beds simply do not work aesthetically in today's landscapes.

- Remember that there are many species of perennials which bloom very early in the spring. Use these interplanted with spring-blooming bulbs and, as in the case of bulbs, consider the planting not only from the outdoor point of view, but from indoors through windows, so that you can enjoy them from inside the house as well as outdoors. Late spring, summer, and fall plantings can be planned strictly from an outside perspective if you wish, since chances are you'll be spending a considerable amount of time in your garden.
- Perennials can be used for splashes of color in distant parts of the garden. Plant large groups of each kind for best visual results, and don't plant symmetrically, rather, try to emulate nature.

When planning a distant planting keep in mind that the hot colors—red, yellow, and orange—will make the planting seem closer to the eye, while the cool colors—blue, purple, and green—recede and appear to be more distant.

Selecting a site. First consider light. Some perennials prefer full sun, some partial sun, and others thrive in deep shade. Consult the individual entries to see which perennials are suitable for each light condition. In addition, a well-drained area is best suited for most kind of perennials you might wish to grow for cut flowers.

PLANNING A PERENNIAL PLANTING. When planning a cut-flower landscape scheme, it is best to work

The Permanent Cut-Flower Collection

The pale yellow flower clusters and leaves of lady's mantle blend well with the white flowering spikes of Veronica *'Alpina Alba' and the feathery red* Astilbe *'Fanal' in both this informal perennial bed and in arrangements.*

Although the red Flanders poppies in this meadow garden do not grow in North America, the 'Plains' coreopsis and 'Oxeye' daisies do, along with many native flowers that are yours for the picking in nearby fields.

it out on graph paper. Using a scale of one inch to every foot of garden space, sketch out the area you wish to plant. Then, keeping the following in mind, give your creative impulse free rein.

- There are advocates of herbaceous, or perennial, borders and those of herbaceous island beds. Borders are the traditional way of installing perennials, deriving from the English gardens of the nineteenth century, when vast fifty-foot-long plantings of perennials provided a spectacle all during the growing season. The only problem

with borders is that to be effective they must be at least six feet deep, preferably eight, and they should have as a backdrop a wall or a tall green hedge. This entails considerable maintenance. In the days of inexpensive labor, gardeners took care of that, but these days most homeowners maintain their gardens themselves. For this reason, island beds—accessible from all sides—are usually preferable. These can be any shape, rectangular, oval, or free-form. However, square or rectangular beds set in the middle of a lawn look particularly ugly during the winter when the garden is bare of bloom and foliage. For most landscaping purposes, it is best to design an informal, free-form island cutting bed, perhaps six to ten or twelve feet across at its widest point. For the most pleasing visual effect the bed should be about three times as long as it is wide and placed off-center in a lawn area. That is, don't set it square in the middle of the lawn. In this way, even though the bed will be bare in winter, it won't be situated so that it is *the* focal point in the yard.

- If you plan a herbaceous cutting garden as a border, the tall plants should be placed in the rear, medium-height plants in the middle, and low-growing types in the front. In an island bed, taller plants belong in the middle, low-growing plants on the edges, and medium-height plants in between.
- Some mail-order houses offer package perennial cutting gardens, already planned for color combinations, gradation of height, and a particular growing condition. These are usually a good investment for someone who has neither the time nor the creative imagination to plan their own.
- Never plant in straight rows, but stagger plantings to achieve an informal effect.
- White-flowering plants are essential to break up color patterns. At least one quarter of your planting should be white. The white flowers will also be very useful in your flower arrangements.
- Consult the individual entries to see what time of year various plants bloom to insure that you have cut-flower material throughout the season. Try to plan your scheme so that there is always something in bloom.

PREPARING THE SOIL. There are perennials which prefer sandy soil, some which will thrive in moisture-laden soil, and some which do best in poor soil. However, as a rule, if you enrich the soil moderately, almost all the perennials described here will thrive and bloom.

Stake out your cut-flower perennial bed and dig to a depth of one foot. Then mix the excavated soil with about one half as much of some organic material such as sphagnum peat moss and/or compost. Then return the mixture to the excavated bed. If the soil is very heavy in clay content, a considerable amount of sand may be added to lighten it. Once

finished, water thoroughly. Do this a week or two in advance of planting your bed.

WHEN TO PLANT. Spring is the best time for most varieties, although most will thrive if planted in early fall. If you do install a fall planting, after the first heavy frost cover the entire planting with a six-inch layer of salt hay mulch to prevent soil heaving from alternate freezing and thawing during the course of the winter.

HOW TO PLANT PERENNIALS. Once you have fortified your soil, designed your cut-flower garden, and purchased the plants, it is time to put in the garden. Bring your chart and a ruler with you. Set the plants where they are to be installed. As a rule, tall-growing plants should be planted two feet apart, medium-height plants eighteen inches apart, low-growing plants twelve inches, and tiny, miniature plants perhaps six inches apart.

One by one, plant the perennials at the same depth at which they were grown in the nursery. If your plants were ordered by mail and arrived bare root, inspect them closely and you will find you can usually see the soil line between the roots and the stems. Plant, firm the soil around the plant, and water thoroughly.

MAINTENANCE. Different species have different needs; however, as a general rule, every year at the beginning of the season work in about one tablespoon of 5-10-5 all-purpose fertilizer around each plant in your garden.

Mulch is a good idea, as it helps keep weeds down and maintains moisture, cutting down on dreary maintenance work. A three- to six-inch mulch of an attractive material such as shredded pine bark or compost is perhaps most effective. There are many mulches available, but some are not recommended. Peat moss should not be used as a mulch as it will form an almost impermeable crust if it dries out. Cocoa bean shells emit a strong chocolate odor, one I think is inappropriate for the garden, and shredded newspaper is ugly. Grass clippings are acceptable (after they've been allowed to dry awhile); however, they tend to leach nitrogen from the soil, requiring an application of a nitrogen-rich fertilizer to compensate for the loss.

Although not all perennials need regular watering, it is a good idea to plan on watering the perennial cut-flower garden thoroughly to a depth of one foot each week during summer drought periods. To lessen the burden of summer watering, reasonably priced hoses with holes punctured in them can be laid down in the garden under the foliage and will be virtually invisible. When watering is necessary you simply let it run for several hours; little water will be lost to evaporation. Also, check each of the individual perennial entries for drought-resistant varieties.

Anemone, Japanese
(Anemone hupehensis japonica)

USDA zones: 5 to 8.
Color: Pink or white with yellow centers.
Description: Single or double blossoms on handsome medium green foliage.
Height: 18 to 48″.
Soil: Moderately fertile.
Light: Partial shade, but will thrive in full sun.
Moisture: Moderately moist.
Planting time: Late spring or early fall. Light frost will not harm newly installed plants.
Distance apart: 18″.
Growing season care: Cut plants to ground after killing frost.
Bloom time: Late summer to early fall.
Length of bloom: 6 to 8 weeks.
Live arrangements: Yes.
Vase life: 4 to 6 days.
Drying: Yes. Hang dry.
Tips: Because it is a late bloomer, Japanese anemone is particularly useful in fall arrangements.

The blossoms are delicate in appearance, rare for species which bloom in the fall. 'Alba' is a white variety, 'Margarete' deep rose, and 'Queen Charlotte' soft pink.

Astilbe

USDA zones: 4 to 8.
Color: White, pink, red, apricot.
Description: Feathery plumes of blossoms on sturdy stems held over medium green foliage.
Height: 12 to 30″.
Soil: Moderately fertile.
Light: Light shade, but will thrive in full sun.
Moisture: Moderately moist.
Planting time: Late spring or early fall. Light frost will not harm recently installed plants.
Distance apart: 2′.
Growing season care: Deadhead after bloom cycle.
Bloom time: Late spring to early summer.
Length of bloom: 3 to 4 weeks.
Live arrangements: Yes.
Vase life: 5 to 7 days.
Drying: Yes. Hang dry.
Tips: Provides soft, feathery texture to arrangements. 'Peach Blossom', a pale salmon-pink variety, is particularly good because of its subtle color.

Baby's Breath
(Gypsophila paniculata and
G. repens rosea)

USDA zones: 3 to 11
Color: *G. paniculata* is white and *G. repens rosea* is pink.
Description: Sprays of tiny flowers on graceful bushlike plants.
Height: 2 to 4′.
Soil: Well-drained, fertile, on the alkaline side.

Light: Full sun.
Moisture: Moderately moist.
Planting time: Late spring or early fall. Light frosts will not harm newly installed plants.
Distance apart: 3'.
Bloom time: Mid- to late summer.
Length of bloom: 6 to 8 weeks.
Live arrangements: Yes.
Vase life: 5 to 7 days.
Drying: Yes. Hang dry.
Tips: If any one plant could be deemed indispensable to the flower arranger, this is it.

Blanketflower
(Gaillardia)

USDA zones: 5 to 8.
Color: Yellow, red, bicolors.
Description: Daisylike blossoms held over handsome medium green foliage.
Height: 12 to 30".
Soil: Ordinary.
Light: Full sun.
Moisture: Very drought resistant. Water only during prolonged summer drought.
Planting time: Late spring or early fall. Light frost does not harm newly installed plants.
Distance apart: 2'.
Growing season care: Deadhead for rebloom.
Bloom time: Midsummer to late fall.
Length of bloom: 8 to 12 weeks.
Live arrangements: Yes.
Vase life: 6 to 10 days.
Drying: Yes. Silica dry.
Tips: Easy to grow, almost carefree. The giant English hybrid 'Dazzler' is yellow and red and 'Burgundy' is an unusual wine red.

Bleeding Heart
(Dicentra)

USDA zones: 3 to 11.
Color: Pink and white, or solid white.
Description: Heart-shaped blossoms held on graceful arching stems over medium green foliage.
Height: 1 to 3'.
Soil: Moderately fertile.
Light: Partial shade.
Moisture: Moderately moist.
Planting time: Midspring is best. Light frost does not harm newly installed plants.
Distance apart: 18".
Growing season care: Remove branches of spent blossoms after bloom to keep tidy. Foliage withers toward the end of summer, so an overplanting of annuals in the garden is recommended.
Bloom time: Midspring.
Length of bloom: 3 to 4 weeks.
Live arrangements: Yes.
Vase life: 4 to 6 days.
Drying: No.
Tips: Blooms in tandem with tulips, azaleas, and dogwood. Adds a graceful elegance to spring bouquets.

Campanula

USDA zones: 3 to 9.
Color: Blue, purple, lavender, white, pink.
Description: Bell- or star-shaped blossoms in clusters or spikes held over attractive medium green to gray foliage.
Height: 6 to 36".
Soil: Moderately fertile.
Light: Full sun or partial shade.
Moisture: Moderately moist.
Planting time: Late spring or early fall. Light frost does not harm newly installed plants.

Campanula carpatica *is only one of scores of species of campanula suitable for arrangements.*

Distance apart: 8″ for low-growing varieties, 18″ for taller ones.

Growing season care: Cut foliage to the ground after killing frost.

Bloom time: Late spring to late summer, depending on species.

Length of bloom: 2 to 4 weeks, depending on variety.

Live arrangements: Yes.

Vase life: 7 to 14 days.

Drying: Yes. Silica dry.

Tips: There are many species to choose from and all are attractive in arrangements. Some recommended species are the tough *C. glomerata* (1 to 3 feet), the elegant *C. persicifolia* (2 to 3½ feet), and the shorter *C. carpatica* (under 1 foot) and *C. garganica* (6 inches).

Chrysanthemum

USDA zones: 5 to 9.

Color: Wide range including yellow, gold, white, rust, orange, red, purple, lavender.

Description: Many blossom shapes, but pompon is perhaps the most readily available. Spider shapes are also effective in arrangements.

Height: 8 to 36″.

Soil: Moderately fertile.

Light: Full sun, but will tolerate semishade.

Moisture: Drought resistant, but water during prolonged summer drought.

Planting time: Mid- to late spring for small transplants; late summer to early fall for nursery-grown mature plants. Light frost will not harm plants.

Distance apart: 18″.

Growing season care: Cut back foliage after killing frost. The following spring, dig up the plant, divide, discard the woody center, and replant the divisions.

Bloom time: Early fall to killing frost and beyond.

Length of bloom: 6 to 8 weeks.

Live arrangements: Yes.

Vase life: 1 to 2 weeks.

Drying: Yes. Hang dry or silica dry.

Tips: After planting, pinch every three weeks until July 4 to encourage branching and more bloom. There are many varieties of chrysanthemums, but some, which are usually greenhouse grown, are not hardy in colder climates. Inquire locally about suitable, hardy species. *C. × morifolium*, commonly called garden mums, are hardy to Zone 5 and sometimes to Zone 4 with a winter protection of a heavy straw mulch.

Clematis

USDA zones: 3 to 11, depending on species.

Color: White, pink, red, blue, yellow, lavender, purple, and combinations thereof, followed by silvery seedpods.

Description: Saucer-shaped blossoms 1 to 9″ in diameter held on vines sporting handsome medium green, glossy foliage.

Length: 3 to 30′.

Soil: Moderately fertile, slightly alkaline.

Light: Prefers roots in the shade, foliage in full sun or partial shade.

Moisture: Keep well-watered during summer drought.

Planting time: Early to late spring is best.

Distance apart: 3′.

Bloom time: Late spring to late fall, depending on species.

Length of bloom: 3 to 4 weeks.

Pruning: This is a complicated business, since some species should be cut back to about 1′ in late winter, and others should merely be pruned to remove dead vines or to shape or contain plant. It is best to check with the nursery or garden center where you buy the plant.

Live arrangements: Yes.

Vase life: 2 to 3 days.

Drying: Blossoms do not dry well; however, seedpods do and add an exotic touch to arrangements.

Tips: When planting, dig a hole 2′ across by 2′ deep. Fortify the soil with substantial amounts of sphagnum peat moss or compost. You do this so that the soil will retain moisture around the roots of the plant, essential to vigorous, healthy growth.

Coneflower, Purple
(Echinacea)

USDA zones: 3 to 9.

Color: Plum-pink or white with orange cone center.

Description: Spidery petals on 3-inch blossoms held over handsome deep green foliage.

Height: 3′.

Soil: Sandy and rich.

Light: Full sun.

Moisture: Drought resistant once established.

Planting time: Early to late spring or late fall. Light frost will not harm newly installed plants.

Distance apart: 2′.

Growing season care: Deadhead for rebloom.

Bloom time: Early summer to killing frost and beyond.

Length of bloom: 6 to 8 weeks.

Live arrangements: Yes.

Vase life: 7 to 14 days.

Drying: No.

Tips: One of the easiest perennials to grow, it is long-lasting in cut-flower arrangements. The best are *E. purpurea* 'WFF Strain' and *E. p.* 'White Swan'.

Coreopsis
(C. grandiflora/lanceolata)

USDA zones: 4 to 11.

Color: Yellow and yellow-mahogany-red combinations.

Description: Daisylike blossoms held over medium green handsome foliage.

Height: 2′.

Soil: Ordinary to poor.

Light: Full sun.

Moisture: Drought resistant, but water during prolonged summer drought.

Planting time: Early to late spring or early fall. Light frost will not harm newly installed plants.
Distance apart: 2'.
Bloom time: Late spring to killing frost.
Length of bloom: 3 to 4 months.
Live arrangements: Yes.
Vase life: 1 to 2 weeks.
Drying: No.
Tips: If quantity of bloom is what you want, this is a good selection. 'Early Sunrise' is floriferous and tidy.

Cushion Spurge
(Euphorbia epithymoides)

USDA zones: 4 to 11.
Color: Bright yellow, chartreuse, and green.
Description: Clusters of florets and leaves over bright green foliage.
Height: 12 to 18".
Soil: Ordinary.
Light: Full sun.
Moisture: Water regularly during prolonged summer drought.
Planting time: Late spring or early fall. Light frost will not harm newly installed plants.
Distance apart: 1'.
Growing season care: Remove dead foliage after killing frost.
Bloom time: Foliage and blossoms offer yellow coloration in midspring. During summer, foliage is an ordinary medium green.
Length of bloom: 3 to 4 weeks.
Live arrangements: Yes, foliage provides lovely notes of chartreuse and yellow.
Vase life: 4 to 5 days.
Drying: No.
WARNING: *Sap of plant is irritating to sensitive skin, causing a rash, but will not cause illness.*

Daisy, Michaelmas
(Aster)

USDA zones: 2 to 8, depending on variety.
Color: Pink, red, blue, violet, white.
Description: Clusters of single daisylike or double pompon blossoms on medium green foliage.
Height: 8 to 24".
Soil: Moderately fertile.
Light: Full sun.
Moisture: Moderately moist.
Planting time: Late spring or early fall. Light frost will not harm newly installed plants.
Distance apart: 18".
Growing season care: Some varieties may need staking. If plant gets rangy provide support.
Bloom time: Late summer to killing frost and beyond.
Length of bloom: 6 to 8 weeks.
Live arrangements: Yes.
Vase life: 7 to 10 days.
Drying: No.
Tips: Taller-growing varieties can become rangy. Dwarfs are better suited to the average garden. These include 'Bonny Blue', 'Pink Bouquet', 'Snow Cushion', and 'Red Star'.

Daisy, Shasta
(Chrysanthemum × superbum)

USDA zones: 5 to 9.
Color: White with yellow centers.
Description: Single or double daisylike blossoms held over handsome deep green foliage.
Height: 12 to 42".
Soil: Moderately fertile.
Light: Full sun or partial shade.
Moisture: Moderately moist.
Planting time: Early spring or early fall. Light frost will not harm newly installed plants.

Another very useful flower in early summer arrangements is the shasta daisy.

Daisy, Transvaal
(Gerbera)

USDA zones: 8 to 11.
Color: All colors except blue.
Description: Daisylike blooms on handsome medium green foliage.
Height: 7 to 24".
Soil: Enriched.
Light: Full sun.
Moisture: Water regularly during prolonged summer drought.
Planting time: After all danger of frost.
Distance apart: 1'.
Growing season care: Deadhead for rebloom.
Bloom time: Early summer to killing frost.
Length of bloom: 2 to 3 months.
Live arrangements: Yes.
Vase life: 1 to 3 weeks.
Drying: Yes. Silica dry.
Tips: Not hardy so treat as an annual in Zones 7 and north. The Rainbow series is tough, fast-growing, and compact with profuse bloom and is available by color.

Distance apart: 1' for miniature varieties, 2' for giants.
Growing season care: Deadhead for rebloom.
Bloom time: Early to late summer.
Length of bloom: 6 to 8 weeks.
Live arrangements: Yes.
Vase life: 3 to 6 days.
Drying: No.
Tips: A wide variety is available, from dwarfs ('Little Miss Muffet') to giants ('Polaris').

Delphinium

USDA zones: 3 to 8.
Color: White, blue, purple, pink, and combinations thereof.
Description: Spikes of florets on loose medium green foliage.
Height: 2 to 7'.
Soil: Very rich.
Light: Full sun or partial shade.
Moisture: Moderately moist.
Planting time: Late spring or early fall, but spring is best. Light frost will not harm newly installed plants.
Distance apart: 2'.

Growing season care: Taller varieties require staking. Deadhead for rebloom.

Bloom time: Late spring to early summer and sometimes a second bloom in early fall.

Length of bloom: 3 to 4 weeks, often twice during the season.

Live arrangements: Yes.

Vase life: 5 to 8 days.

Drying: Yes. Silica dry.

Tips: Can be difficult to grow unless conditions are ideal, but because of their spectacular beauty in arrangements, they are well worth the effort. If you do not have luck with delphiniums, substitute easy-to-grow annual larkspur (see page 50), which, although not as spectacular, will create a similar vertical effect in an arrangement. Species delphiniums *D.* × *belladonna* and *D.* × *b.* 'Bellamosa' are easier to grow than Pacific Coast hybrids of Blackmore and Langdon strains.

Digitalis adds soaring vertical lines to late-spring arrangements.

Foxglove
(Digitalis grandiflora)

USDA zones: 3 to 11.

Color: All colors except blue.

Description: Spikes of pitcher-shaped florets held on long stalks over medium green rosettes of foliage. Biennial.

Height: 1½ to 5'.

Soil: Ordinary, well-drained.

Light: Partial shade, but will thrive in full sun.

Moisture: Water regularly throughout growing season.

Planting time: Since foxglove is a biennial, start outdoors from seed after all danger of frost has passed. Plant will not bloom first year, but will winter over and bloom the second year.

Distance apart: 1'.

Growing season care: Deadhead for rebloom.

Bloom time: Late spring.

Length of bloom: 3 to 4 weeks.

Live arrangements: Yes.

Vase life: 5 to 10 days.

Drying: No.

Tips: Easily grown from seed. *D. purpurea* 'Alba', a white variety, is particularly beautiful.

WARNING: *If you use this for indoor arrangements, keep in mind that seeds and all parts of the plant are poisonous to dogs, cats, and human beings if eaten, and can be fatal!*

Gayfeather
(Liatris)

USDA zones: 3 to 11.
Color: Rose-purple or white.
Description: Spikes of feathery blossoms held on tall stems over handsome spiked green foliage.
Height: 2 to 3'.
Soil: Ordinary.
Light: Full sun.
Moisture: Moderately moist.
Planting time: Midspring or early fall. Light frost will not harm newly installed plants.
Distance apart: 18".
Growing season care: Deadhead to keep tidy. Cut foliage to the ground after killing frost.
Bloom time: Early to midsummer.
Length of bloom: 4 to 6 weeks.
Live arrangements: Yes.
Vase life: 6 to 10 days.
Drying: Yes. Silica dry.
Tips: A native American wildflower which adapts very well to the garden and makes a lovely addition to cut-flower arrangements.

Goatsbeard
(Aruncus)

USDA zones: 3 to 8.
Color: Cream.
Description: Loose, feathery panicles of blossoms held over medium green foliage. Shrublike in appearance.
Height: 4 to 6'.
Soil: Slightly enriched.
Light: Semishade.
Moisture: Likes moisture, so water regularly or plant in a wet area.
Planting time: Early spring or early fall. Light frost will not harm newly installed plants.

Feathery goatsbeard is useful in softening spring arrangements.

Distance apart: 3'.
Growing season care: Deadhead to keep tidy. Cut foliage to the ground after killing frost or in early spring before new growth starts.
Bloom time: Late spring.
Length of bloom: 2 to 3 weeks.
Live arrangements: Yes.
Vase life: 4 to 6 days.
Drying: Yes. Hang dry.
Tips: Although technically a herbaceous perennial, this plant is too large for small gardens. Use as you would a shrub.

Hellebore
(Helleborus)

USDA zones: 3 to 8.
Color: Maroon, pink, or red to pale green, white, and cream.
Description: 2" cup-shaped blossoms held on low-growing, evergreen foliage.

Height: 1 to 2'.
Soil: Rich loam.
Light: Partial shade.
Moisture: Moderately moist.
Planting time: Mid- to late spring or early fall, although spring is preferred. Light frost will not harm newly installed plants.
Distance apart: 18".
Growing season care: Deadhead to keep tidy.
Bloom time: Late winter to early spring.
Length of bloom: 3 to 4 weeks.
Live arrangements: Yes.
Vase life: 1 to 2 weeks.
Drying: Yes. Hang dry.
Tips: The earliest of all blooming perennials. Useful in arrangements with early spring bulbs and forced shrub cuttings.
WARNING: *If you use this for indoor arrangements, keep in mind that seeds and all parts of the plant are poisonous to dogs, cats, and human beings if eaten, and can be fatal!*

Hellebores are among the earliest perennials to bloom and for that reason are a must in any cut-flower garden.

Hosta

USDA zones: 3 to 9.
Color: White, lilac, pale lavender.
Description: Delicate blossom spikes on lush foliage in colors ranging from yellow to dark green, gray and near steel blue, often edged or speckled with white, cream, or yellow. Leaf texture varies from smooth, to ribbed, to quilted.
Height: From several inches to 4'.
Soil: Rich, but will thrive in ordinary.
Light: Semishade, but will thrive in deep shade or full sun.
Moisture: Moist conditions, but will thrive in dry climates.
Planting time: Early spring or late fall. Light frost will not harm newly installed plants.
Distance apart: 2'.
Growing season care: Deadhead to keep tidy.
Bloom time: Early to late summer, depending on variety. Foliage from late spring through late fall.
Length of bloom: 2 to 3 weeks.
Live arrangements: Yes, particularly the foliage.
Vase life: 5 to 7 days.
Drying: No.
Tips: 'Honeybells' offers a particularly lovely light fragrance. The Japanese have been using the flamboyant hosta foliage in arrangements for centuries.

Iris, Bearded or German

USDA zones: 3 to 8.
Color: All but green.
Description: 6 to 8" blossoms with standards and falls.
Height: 1½ to 4'.
Soil: Well-drained, ordinary.
Light: Full sun, but will bloom in partial shade.
Moisture: Drought resistant, but water regularly during prolonged summer drought.

Bearded or German iris must be used carefully in arrangements because of their flamboyant shape and colors.

Planting time: August and September are best; however, can be planted anytime during the growing season.

Distance apart: 1'.

Growing season care: Deadhead to keep tidy.

Bloom time: Late spring to early summer. Newly introduced reblooming varieties also bloom in early fall.

Length of bloom: 2 to 3 weeks.

Live arrangements: Yes.

Vase life: 2 to 5 days.

Drying: No.

Tips: Bearded iris are utterly spectacular in the garden, but because they are so large, they can be difficult to work with in arrangements. Unless you are so taken with them and wish to create large arrangements with many iris stalks, use one or two of the softer-colored varieties mixed with an abundance of smaller blossoms.

Iris, Siberian
(Iris sibirica)

USDA zones: 3 to 8.

Color: Blue, purple, white, yellow, or combinations thereof.

Description: 3″ blooms with standards and small falls.

Height: 1½ to 3'.

Soil: Well-drained, ordinary.

Light: Full sun, but will bloom in partial shade.

Moisture: Drought resistant, but water regularly during prolonged summer drought.

Planting time: Mid- to late spring or early fall. Light frost will not harm newly installed plants.

Distance apart: 1'.

Growing season care: Let spent flowers remain on stalks as the dried pods are particularly attractive in fall arrangements.

Bloom time: Late spring.

Length of bloom: 2 to 3 weeks.

Live arrangements: Yes.

Vase life: 2 to 6 days.

Drying: Yes, but only the seedpods. Blossoms do not dry well.

Tips: Siberian iris add subtle vertical lines to cut-flower arrangements.

Ivy
(Hedera)

USDA zones: 3 to 9, depending on variety.

Color: Grown for evergreen foliage which is deep, medium or light green, often variegated, depending on variety.

Description: Vinelike, heart-shaped foliage.

Length: To 25' if allowed to climb.

Soil: Ordinary.

Light: Deep shade to full sun.

Moisture: Drought resistant, but water regularly

during prolonged summer drought.

Planting time: Early spring or fall. Light frost will not harm newly installed plants.

Distance apart: 2'.

Growing season care: Prune in fall to keep in bounds.

Live arrangements: Yes.

Vase life: Several weeks.

Drying: No.

Tips: Use the lush, deep green foliage to provide graceful lines in arrangements.

Lady's Mantle
(*Alchemilla mollis*)

USDA zones: 3 to 7.

Color: Yellow-green.

Description: Panicles of blossoms held over lobed foliage resembling that of water lilies.

Height: 1 to 1½'.

Soil: Enrich slightly.

Light: Full sun or partial shade.

Moisture: Water regularly during prolonged summer drought.

Planting time: Early to late spring. Light frost will not harm newly installed plants.

Distance apart: 18".

Growing season care: Deadhead blossoms and cut foliage to the ground after killing frost.

Bloom time: Early summer.

Length of bloom: 3 to 4 weeks.

Live arrangements: Yes.

Vase life: 4 to 6 days.

Drying: No.

Tips: These yellow-green blossoms are stunning and exotic in indoor arrangements.

This extravagant lupine garden at Mount Congreve, County Waterford, Ireland, offers a basketful of blossoms in a rainbow of colors for indoor arrangements.

Lupine
(*Lupinus*)

USDA zones: 4 to 9.

Color: All colors.

Description: Dramatic spikes of pealike blooms held on erect spikes over medium green foliage.

Height: 1 to 3'.

Soil: Ordinary, but lime free; lupines hate alkaline soil.

Light: Sun or partial shade.

Moisture: Moderately moist.

Planting time: Late spring or early fall. Light frost will not harm newly installed plants.

Distance apart: 2'.
Growing season care: Deadhead to keep tidy.
Bloom time: Late spring to early summer.
Length of bloom: 3 to 4 weeks.
Live arrangements: Yes.
Vase life: 5 to 7 days.
Drying: No.
Tips: Lupines are a touch flamboyant; however, the subtler colored varieties add dramatic flair to cut-flower arrangements. Select the Russell strain hybrids.
WARNING: *If you use this for indoor arrangements, keep in mind that seeds and all parts of the plant are poisonous to dogs, cats, and human beings if eaten, and can be fatal!*

Peony
(Paeonia)

USDA zones: 3 to 8.
Color: Pink, white, red, yellow, or combinations thereof.

Single peonies are less overpowering in arrangements than the common double variety.

Description: Immense single or double pompon blossoms held on sturdy stems over rich dark green foliage which remains attractive throughout the season.
Height: 2 to 4'.
Soil: Well-enriched.
Light: Full sun.
Moisture: Moderately moist.
Planting time: Plant only in August.
Distance apart: 3'.
Growing season care: Deadhead to keep tidy. Cut foliage to the ground after killing frost, as disease can be harbored there over winter.
Bloom time: Late spring.
Length of bloom: 3 to 4 weeks.
Live arrangements: Yes.
Vase life: 7 to 10 days.
Drying: No.
Tips: Useful in large, flamboyant arrangements.

Phlox
(Phlox carolina/paniculata)

USDA zones: 3 to 9.
Color: White, pink, purple, red, lavender, orange.
Description: Large flower heads composed of individual florets held on stiff stalks over medium green foliage.
Height: 4'.
Soil: Moderately fertile.
Light: Full sun.
Moisture: Moderately moist.
Planting time: Early to late spring or fall. Light frost will not harm newly installed plants.
Distance apart: 2'.
Growing season care: Deadhead to prevent formation of seeds, which self-sow and can be a nuisance. They also are not true to their parentage but rather sport common unattractive magenta blossoms. Cut foliage to the ground after killing frost.

Bloom time: Early summer to late fall.
Length of bloom: 3 to 4 months.
Live arrangements: Yes.
Vase life: 5 to 10 days.
Drying: No.
Tips: Plant is subject to mildew, so plant in an area where air circulation is good, or spray with a fungicide according to the manufacturer's instructions. Mildew-resistant, old-fashioned varieties have recently become available. Some of these are *P. carolina* 'Miss Lingard' (white), and *P. c.* 'Rosalinde' (lilac-pink). White Flower Farm offers them.

Garden Pinks
(Dianthus × allwoodii and many others)

USDA zones: 3 to 9.
Color: White, pink, red, or combinations thereof.
Description: Single or double pompon-type blossoms on elegant bluish green or gray-green foliage.
Height: 8 to 18″.
Soil: Sandy loam.
Light: Full sun or partial shade.
Moisture: Drought resistant, but water regularly during prolonged summer drought.
Planting time: Mid- to late spring or early fall. Light frost will not harm newly installed plants.
Distance apart: 1′.
Growing season care: Deadhead to keep tidy.
Bloom time: Late spring, with some varieties sporting a second bloom in early fall.
Length of bloom: 3 to 4 weeks.
Live arrangements: Yes.
Vase life: 7 to 12 days.
Drying: Yes. Silica dry.
Tips: All pinks offer a lovely clovelike fragrance.

Their blossoms soften arrangements and are particularly useful in miniature arrangements.

Poppy, Oriental
(Papaver orientale)

USDA zones: 5 to 9.
Color: White, scarlet, orange, pink, or peach, sometimes blotched with black and combinations thereof.
Description: Large cup-shaped blossoms over insignificant foliage.
Height: 2 to 3′.
Soil: Ordinary.
Light: Full sun.
Moisture: Drought resistant.
Planting time: Early spring. Light frost will not harm newly installed plants.
Distance apart: 18″.
Growing season care: Cut back foliage when it dries during midsummer.
Bloom time: Late spring.
Length of bloom: 2 to 3 weeks.
Live arrangements: Yes, spectacular but very short-lived.
Vase life: 2 to 4 days.
Drying: No.
Tips: For arrangements, be sure to sear the ends of the stems immediately after cutting. Overplant with annuals, since the foliage disappears during the summer. If the bright reds and oranges don't suit your needs, select the pale salmon-pink 'Princess Victoria Louise'.

Rose Campion

(Lychnis coronaria)

USDA zones: 4 to 8.
Color: Cerise.
Description: 1½" blossoms on silver-gray, woolly-textured foliage.
Height: 2 to 3'.
Soil: Ordinary.
Light: Full sun.
Moisture: Drought resistant.
Planting time: Mid- to late spring or early fall. Light frost does not harm newly intalled plants.
Distance apart: 18".
Growing season care: Deadhead for rebloom.
Bloom time: Early summer to early fall.
Length of bloom: 8 to 10 weeks.
Live arrangements: Yes.
Vase life: 5 to 7 days.

Although morning glories are not suitable for cutting, Sedum 'Autumn Joy' offers cream-colored blossoms which turn soft pink, useful in late summer arrangements.

Drying: No.
Tips: Rose campion's silver foliage is particularly useful in arrangements.

Sedum 'Autumn Joy'

USDA zones: 3 to 11.
Color: Mauve-pink, turning to brilliant rust.
Description: Compact 3" flower heads held over lush, succulent, jade green foliage.
Height: 2 to 3'.
Soil: Ordinary.
Light: Full sun.
Moisture: Drought resistant.
Planting time: Early spring or fall. Light frost will not harm newly installed plants.
Distance apart: 2'.
Growing season care: At end of season cut the foliage to the ground.
Bloom time: Midsummer to killing frost.

Later in the season, the flower heads of Sedum 'Autumn Joy' turn a deep rust, working well in dried arrangements.

Length of bloom: 6 to 8 weeks.
Live arrangements: Yes.
Vase life: 2 to 3 weeks.
Drying: Yes. Hang dry.
Tips: For drying, wait until the florets turn rust color. It's easy to propagate sedum; simply cut stalks of it in midsummer and stick them in the ground to root.

Sweet William
(Dianthus barbatus)

USDA zones: 3 to 9.
Color: Deep red, white, pink, mauve, lavender, many with white eyes.
Description: 4 to 5″ mounds of clove-scented florets held over deep green foliage. Biennial.
Height: 1 to 2′.
Soil: Ordinary.
Light: Full sun.
Moisture: Moderately moist.
Planting time: Since sweet William is a biennial, start outdoors from seed after all danger of frost has passed. Plant will not bloom the first year, but will winter over and bloom the second year.
Distance apart: 18″.
Growing season care: Deadhead for rebloom.
Bloom time: Late spring to early summer.
Length of bloom: 4 to 8 weeks.
Live arrangements: Yes.
Vase life: 7 to 12 days.
Drying: No.
Tips: It's worth waiting an extra year for this favorite old-fashioned biennial to bloom. The lush flower heads, with their heady clove fragrance, are very useful in arrangements.

Violet
(Viola odorata)

USDA zones: 3 to 9.
Color: Blue, purple, white, or bluish rose.
Description: Familiar pansylike blossoms on glossy, deep green, heart-shaped foliage.
Height: 6 to 8″.
Soil: Enriched but will thrive in average.
Light: Semishade, but will thrive in full sun.
Moisture: Moist.
Planting time: Plant seeds or root divisions in early spring or fall.
Distance apart: 1′.
Length of bloom: Mid- to late spring.
Live arrangements: Yes.
Vase life: 4 to 7 days.
Drying: No.
Tips: Pick when fully open. Spray daily with water to keep blossoms moist.

Wisteria, Japanese/Chinese
(Wisteria floribunda/sinensis)

USDA zones: 4 to 9.
Color: White, purple, lavender, or pink.
Description: Fragrant flower clusters, 9 to 20″ long, on vigorous growing vines with medium green, loosely structured foliage.
Height/length: To 50′.
Soil: Moderately fertile, acidic.
Light: Full sun.
Moisture: Keep well-watered during summer drought.
Planting time: Early spring.
Distance apart: 10′.
Bloom time: Late spring to early summer.
Length of bloom: 2 to 3 weeks.
Pruning: Must be heavily pruned every spring to keep plant within bounds, particularly if planted

White-flowering wisteria offers a bonanza of cutting material in midspring. Their weeping quality is particularly effective in dramatic, grandiose arrangements.

on a trellis or pergola adjoining a house or near trees. Wisteria has been known to grow its way into attics and can literally destroy a house if allowed to grow unchecked.

Live arrangements: Yes.

Vase life: 5 to 7 days.

Drying: No.

Tips: A highly fragrant, very fast grower.

Yarrow

(Achillea)

USDA zones: 3 to 8.

Color: Yellow, gold, white, pink, and shades of red, purple, or peach, depending on variety.

Description: Tightly structured flower heads held over fernlike foliage.

Height: 3 to 48".

Soil: Moderately fertile, but tolerates sandy soil.

Light: Full sun.

Moisture: Drought resistant once established.

Planting time: Early spring or fall. Frosts will not harm newly installed plants.

Growing season care: Deadhead spent blooms to encourage second or third bloom. Taller varieties may need staking.

Bloom time: Early summer to late fall.

Length of bloom: 6 to 8 weeks.

Live arrangements: Yes.

Vase life: 10 to 14 days.

Drying: Yes. Hang dry.

Tips: Yarrow retains color very well when dried and, in fact, is more effective in dried arrangements than in live ones.

Ferns

Ferns are very useful in creating arrangements, softening the blowsier blossoms, and adding lacy texture to small arrangements.

Japanese Painted Fern
(Athyrium goeringianum 'Pictum')

USDA zones: 5 to 8.

Description: Coarse gray-green and red foliage.

Height: 1'.

Soil: Enriched, with a considerable amount of organic matter.

Light: Partial shade; full sun bleaches out color.

Lady fern is especially attractive for use in summer arrangements.

Moisture: Moderately moist.

Planting time: Early to midspring is best. Light frost will not harm newly installed plants.

Distance apart: 1'.

Growing season care: Cut back spent foliage at end of season.

Live arrangements: Yes.

Vase life: Variable, to 14 days.

Drying: No.

Tips: The gray-green and red foliage is appropriate for some arrangements, but not all.

Lady Fern
(Athyrium filix-femina)

USDA zones: 5 to 8.

Description: Bright, yellow-green, deep-cut leaves.

Height: 2 to 4'.

Soil: Ordinary.

Light: Partial shade.

Moisture: Moderately moist.

Planting time: Early to midspring is best. Light frost will not harm newly installed plants.

Distance apart: 2'.

Growing season care: Cut back spent foliage at end of season.

Live arrangements: Yes.

Vase life: Variable, to 14 days.

Drying: No.

Tips: Useful in both live and dried bouquets to add different textures.

Ostrich Fern
(Matteuccia struthiopteris)

USDA zones: 5 to 8.

Description: Feathery yellow-green fronds.

Height: 3 to 6'.

Soil: Enriched with organic matter.

The stately ostrich fern adds vertical lines to large arrangements.

Light: Deep to light shade.
Moisture: Moderately moist.
Planting time: Early to midspring is best. Light frost will not harm newly installed plants.
Distance apart: 3'.
Growing season care: Cut back spent foliage at end of season.
Live arrangements: Yes.
Vase life: Variable, to 14 days.
Drying: No.
Tips: These large fronds add dramatic touches to large arrangements.

Royal Fern
(Osmunda regalis)

USDA zones: 5 to 8.
Description: Large, smooth, deep forest green fronds.
Height: 4 to 6'.

Soil: Slightly acid.
Light: Deep to light shade.
Moisture: Moderately moist.
Planting time: Early to midspring is best. Light frost will not hurt newly installed plants.
Distance apart: 3'.
Growing season care: Cut back spent foliage at end of season.
Live arrangements: Yes.
Vase life: Variable, to 14 days.
Drying: No.
Tips: Like the ostrich fern, it can be useful in large arrangements.

Herbs

Artemisia

USDA zones: 5 to 9.
Description: Feathery silver foliage with white seedheads.
Height: 1 to 3'.
Soil: Well-drained, ordinary.
Light: Full sun, but will grow in partial shade.
Moisture: Water only during prolonged summer drought, as too much moisture rots the foliage.
Planting time: Late spring or fall.
Distance apart: 18".
Growing season care: Divide every 2 years.
Live arrangements: Yes.
Vase life: 2 to 3 weeks.
Drying: Yes. Hang dry.
Tips: Artemisia's foliage can be used for color and texture contrast in arrangements. I recommend *A. albula* 'Silver King', *A. ludoviciana* var. *albula* 'Silver Queen', and *A. schmidtiana* 'Silver Mound'.

The soft silver-gray foliage of lamb's ears is always a welcome touch in small arrangements.

Betony or Lamb's Ears
(Stachys)

USDA zones: 4 to 9.
Color: Purple flowers.
Description: A low mat of woolly, silvery white foliage with unattractive flower stalks.
Height: Foliage, 6″; flower stalks 12 to 18″.
Soil: Well-drained, ordinary.
Light: Full sun, but will grow in partial shade.
Moisture: Water only during prolonged summer drought, as too much moisture rots the foliage.
Planting time: Late spring or fall.
Distance apart: 18″.
Growing season care: Since flower stalks are ugly, most gardeners remove them. Divide every 2 years.
Live arrangements: Yes.
Vase life: 5 to 7 days.

Drying: Yes. Hang dry.
Tips: The woolly textured leaves offer interest to miniature summer arrangements.

Feverfew
(Chrysanthemum parthenium)

USDA zones: 4 to 9.
Color: White with yellow centers.
Description: Light green leaves with daisylike blossoms held on long stems.
Height: 18 to 24″.
Soil: Well-drained.
Light: Full sun but tolerates partial shade; however, flowering is less likely.
Moisture: Water only during prolonged summer drought.
Planting time: Late spring, after all danger of frost.
Distance apart: 2′.
Growing season care: If conditions are favorable, it will self-sow prodigiously, but is easy to control by pulling up the unwanted plants.
Bloom time: Mid- to late summer.
Length of bloom: 6 to 8 weeks.
Live arrangements: Yes.
Vase life: 2 to 3 weeks.
Drying: Yes. Silica dry.
Tips: These small flowers add delicate softening touches to arrangements with larger flowers.

Lavender
(Lavandula)

USDA zones: 6 to 9, although may survive if well-protected during the winter in the southern stretches of Zone 5. Farther north, treat as an annual.

Color: Lavender, white, pink.

Description: Narrow, silvery gray, 2″ long leaves with tiny blossoms.

Height: *Lavandula angustifolia* grows to 4′. Lower-growing, more manageable varieties include 'Hidcote' (12″), 'Munstead' (18″), and 'Compacta' (10″).

Soil: Sandy with good drainage.

Light: Full sun, but will grow in partial shade.

Moisture: Water only during extended summer drought.

Planting time: Mid- to late spring or early fall. Light frost will not hurt newly installed plants.

Distance apart: 18″.

Growing season care: If plant becomes leggy after flowering, cut back.

Bloom time: Midsummer to early fall.

Length of bloom: 6 to 8 weeks.

Live arrangements: Yes.

Vase life: 7 to 14 days.

Drying: Yes. Hang dry.

Tips: One of the classic old-fashioned flowers for arrangements. And, they offer that irresistible lavender scent.

Southernwood
(Artemisia abrotanum)

USDA zones: 4 to 9.

Color: Pale yellow.

Description: Feathery, gray-green leaves with small blossoms.

Height: 2 to 4′.

Soil: Well-drained, average.

Light: Full sun.

Moisture: Drought resistant, but water regularly during extended summer drought.

Planting time: Spring, after all danger of frost has passed.

Distance apart: 3′.

Growing season care: Trim each year to keep the plant tidy. Divide every 3 to 4 years.

Bloom time: Blossoms from mid- to late summer; foliage from late spring to killing frost.

Length of bloom: 2 to 4 weeks.

Live arrangements: Yes. Use foliage, remove flowers.

Vase life: 7 to 14 days.

Drying: Yes. Hang dry foliage. Remove flowers.

Tips: Feathery foliage is particularly effective to soften arrangements.

Ornamental Grasses

Ornamental grasses add so much to arrangements both live and dried because of their interesting textures.

This ornamental grass garden offers a near endless supply of cutting material.

Japanese Blood Grass
(Imperata cylindrica)

USDA zones: 6 to 9.

Description: Erect, pointed leaves with glowing red tips.

Height: 1 to 2'.

Soil: Tolerates poor soil.

Light: Plant has most color when planted in partial shade.

Moisture: Drought resistant, but water regularly during prolonged summer drought.

Planting time: Mid- to late spring is best. Light frost will not harm newly installed plants.

Distance apart: 18".

Growing season care: Cut foliage to the ground before spring growth commences.

Live arrangements: Yes.

Vase life: Variable, to 2 weeks.

Drying: Yes. Hang dry.

Tips: Blood grass's foliage combines particularly well with dried seedpods gathered in the wild.

Pampas Grass, Compact
(Cortaderia selloana 'Pumila')

USDA zones: 7 to 11.

Color: White and pink.

Description: 3' long, silky, plume panicles held over tall, clump-forming, upright grass with bluish foliage.

Height: 4 to 6'.

Soil: Ordinary.

Light: Full sun.

Moisture: Drought resistant, but water regularly during prolonged summer drought.

Planting time: Spring or fall.

Distance apart: 3'.

Growing season care: Cut foliage to ground before spring growth commences.

Live arrangements: Yes.

Vase life: Variable, to 2 weeks.

Drying: Yes. Hang dry.

Tips: Very large plumes add spectacular touches to large dried or live arrangements.

Rose Fountain Grass
(Pennisetum alopecuroides)

USDA zones: 6 to 9.

Description: Rose-tan foxtail-shaped spikelets; very fine arching foliage.

Height: 3 to 4'.

Soil: Well-drained, ordinary.

Light: Full sun.

Moisture: Drought resistant, but water regularly during prolonged summer drought.

Rose fountain grass (Pennisetum alopecuroides) takes on a golden hue in the fall garden and is particularly effective when used in arrangements with autumn-blooming chrysanthemums.

The lush plumes of silver banner grass can also be dried for winter arrangements.

Planting time: Mid- to late spring is best. Light frost will not harm newly installed plants.

Distance apart: 3'.

Growing season care: Cut foliage to the ground before spring growth commences.

Live arrangements: Yes.

Vase life: Variable, to 2 weeks.

Drying: Yes. Hang dry.

Tips: Useful in both live and dried arrangements to add different textures.

Silver Banner Grass

(Miscanthus sacchariflorus)

USDA zones: 5 to 9.

Description: Broad grassy leaves with silvery-tan plumes.

Height: 4 to 5'.

Soil: Ordinary.

Light: Partial shade but tolerates full sun.

Moisture: Drought resistant, but water regularly during prolonged summer drought.

Planting time: Mid- to late spring or fall. Light frost will not harm newly installed plants.

Distance apart: 3'.

Growing season care: Cut foliage to the ground before spring growth commences.

Live arrangements: Yes.

Vase life: Variable, to 2 weeks.

Drying: Yes. Hang dry.

Tips: Plumes are especially attractive in large dried or live arrangements.

9

Roses

· · ·

If it could be said that there is one flower which is the all-time favorite of flower arrangers, it would certainly be the rose. And surely there is a place for a rosebush of some kind in every cut-flower garden, and for all zones in North America.

When you select rose varieties for the cutting garden, be sure to keep the following in mind:

• *Profusion of bloom.* You will want to be sure to have an abundance of cutting material. Some rosebushes, such as floribundas, climbers, and the new English roses from hybridizer David Austin offer profuse bloom. Although hybrid tea roses are stunning, they do not offer as much cutting material as these other types of rosebushes

• *Fragrance.* Many of today's hybrid teas bear little, if any scent. Some do, however, so if fragrance is important to you, select those hybrid teas which are heavily scented, or choose floribundas, English roses, or old-fashioned damask and cabbage roses, most of which offer heavy scent.

• *Colors that dry well.* Since you will probably want to dry some blossoms for dried arrangements, be aware that some colors dry better than others. As a general rule, red, yellow, and orange roses retain their brilliant colors the best. White roses turn an ugly brown when dried, and pink turns an undistinguished pale pinkish brown.

• *Include miniature roses.* These are enchanting in miniature arrangements and since the blossoms can be dried whole, they also add captivating touches to dried cut-flower arrangements.

The popular climbing rose 'America' offers an abundance of roses for arrangements and also dresses up any garden.

pale or thick canes. Avoid these as they have been neglected in the nursery. Finally, if there are any swellings, strange dark colors, or growths on the canes and roots, avoid them, as disease is probably present.

TIME OF YEAR TO PLANT. Roses shipped by mail-order nurseries almost always are sent at the proper planting time for your area, usually in midspring. Bushes available at nurseries and garden centers are usually also sold and stocked at the appropriate planting time.

WHERE TO PLANT ROSES. Roses are not fussy about planting sites; however, they do require between four and six hours of sunlight a day, depending on variety, and prefer light in the morning, so an eastern exposure is the best. A dappled-shade southern exposure, or a full-sun northern or western exposure is also satisfactory. Roses like a site with good drainage and adequate air circulation in order to prevent disease.

PLANTING. To plant all varieties except miniatures,

'Blaze' is another prolific bloom which is indispensable for the flower arranger.

BUYING ROSEBUSHES. You can order roses by mail as there are many reputable suppliers in the United States, and you can almost always count on receiving healthy, vigorous plants. If you buy from a nursery or garden center, here's what to look for. First check for grade number. Roses are rated 1, 1½, and 2, with 1 the highest rating and the most expensive. Ratings are determined by size and number of canes. Sometimes a number 2 grade rosebush will produce excellent roses, although usually it takes a few more years, and more care and feeding than a 1 or 1½. But you would do well to buy only number 1 grade roses, in order to ensure that you have the best possible stock to start out with. Second, check to see if the bushes have

Roses

dig a hole about two feet across by 1½ feet deep. For miniatures a one-foor-deep by one-foot-across hole is sufficient. Although they are not fussy about soil, whether the soil is heavy or clay or sand, mix compost, sphagnum peat moss, or some other organic matter in with the soil removed from the hole at a ratio of about two parts soil to one part additive. If drainage is poor, fill the bottom of the hole with rocks or broken flowerpot shards.

Then fashion a cone in the bottom of the hole with some of the soil mixture. If plants are bare root, remove damaged, dried-out, or overly long roots with pruning shears. Position the plant in the hole so that the roots fall over the cone and the graft (the knobby growth just above the roots) is even or just below soil level in zones 4 and 5 or above the soil level in zones 6 to 9. Fill in the soil several inches at a time, tamping it firmly, until the soil level around the rose is even with the surrounding area. Water thoroughly to remove air pockets in the soil.

Some rosebushes are sold in ready-to-plant boxes or containers. There are two schools of thought on planting these. The mail-order nursery's instructions indicate that it is not necessary to remove the paper carton in which the rose is planted; the paper will simply rot. Others feel that it is perhaps better to remove the carton and spread the roots out somewhat before planting. The choice is yours.

SPACING. Hybrid teas, English roses, grandiflora, floribunda, and most old-fashioned roses should be spaced about two feet apart from the center of the bush. Miniatures should be sited about 1½ feet apart, and climbers along fences should be six to eight feet apart or on trellises about four feet apart.

WATERING. As a rule, water thoroughly once a week in the morning so that the soil is soaked to a depth of one to 1½ feet deep. If you place an empty coffee can within the watering area, when there is one inch of water in the bottom, you can assume that the soil has been soaked to the required depth. Of course humidity, rainfall, and the use of mulch can affect this schedule. Use common sense. Overhead watering can be employed if you spray your roses regularly with a fungicide. However, it is perhaps best to invest in a hose which seeps water into the ground. These are available at garden centers and nurseries and are quite inexpensive. In this way you will discourage the growth of fungus diseases. If you do water with a regular hose, try to avoid wetting the leaves.

FERTILIZING. Products specifically labeled "rose fertilizer" are the best. Ortho sells a product which is a combination fertilizer–systemic pest killer–weed killer. It is available at most garden centers and nurseries. You can save yourself a substantial amount of maintenance if you use it. Apply it three times during the season according to the instructions on the package. If you use other products, follow label instructions.

PESTS AND DISEASES. Roses are subject to some pests and diseases, but these are easily controlled. Floribunda, old-fashioned roses, and the new English roses are more pest and disease resistant than the hybrid teas, grandifloras, and climbing roses whose parentage is hybrid tea or grandiflora.

As a preventive, early in spring, before leaf growth starts, spray all the bushes with a dormant oil spray, available at garden centers and nurseries, according to the manufacturer's instructions. You do this to smother any insects and fungi which may have survived the winter.

Three diseases may attack your plants and affect the quality of the flowers. They are:

Rust. This manifests itself in small, powdery orange spots which appear on leaf undersides, ultimately causing the leaves to die. Severe infestation can result in the plant dying.

Powdery mildew. This white powdery substance appears on stems and buds, and can, if allowed to spread, cause the plant to die.

Black spot. This begins with small, black circles which appear first on leaf undersides, then spread to entire leaf, weakening the plant and ultimately causing it to die.

At the first sign of problems, spray with Funginex, an Ortho product, recommended by the American Rose Society, according to the instructions on the bottle. As a preventive it is a good idea to apply this spray while the plants are dormant and then once a week during the growing season, particularly after heavy rains. As another preventive measure, water roses only in the morning, so that the moisture will evaporate during the day and not leave the foliage wet, which leads to disease.

Insects such as aphids, spider mites, and thrips are best controlled with a systemic insect killer. Systemics, which are absorbed into the plant and kill insects on contact, are preferred, because they do not leave unsightly residues on the blossoms and buds which you wish to dry. Japanese beetles are best controlled by handpicking. If you're facing an infestation of epidemic proportions, a Japanese beetle trap, available at most garden centers or nurseries, is recommended.

MULCHING. Mulching your roses is a good idea because it helps to retain moisture and reduces weed growth. Although there are many different kinds of mulches available, either homemade compost or shredded pine or cedar bark is best for rose plantings.

PRUNING. In the fall, when roses stop blooming and go into dormancy, prune only the tallest branches to about three feet high. This is to prevent winter winds from damaging plants. If there are any rose hips (seedpods) left on the bushes, cut them, dry them in a basket, store and when ready, use them in holiday arrangements.

Spring is the time for the annual pruning, but different kinds of roses require different techniques. However, if you follow these general rules, you should have success.

- Wait until new growth begins, when buds begin to emerge from the canes.
- Prune out dead canes to the crown (the base of the plant). Dead canes will be brown or black and dried out. Use sharp pruning shears, loppers, or a small saw to do this.
- Prune out frost-damaged canes to healthy wood, which is white or light green all the way through the cane.
- Make all pruning cuts at an angle about one third of an inch above a bud which faces away from the center of the bush.
- Open the center of the bush, that is, prune out thin twigs and stems near the middle. This is particularly important with floribunda varieties.
- Prune out suckers emerging from below the graft, the knobby growth at the base of the plant. Such suckers would grow from the rootstock and not produce blooms true to the variety you have planted.
- Thin out all but 4 to 7 canes. Those left should be at least as thick as a pencil. For a more abundant supply of roses, prune these canes to two feet. The flowers will be smaller, but there will be more of them.
- When finished, apply Elmer's glue or shellac to all exposed cuts to prevent moisture evaporation and insect infestation.

PRUNING CLIMBERS. Climbers require a few special techniques. Most form flowering laterals, that is, side shoots from the main branches. In spring cut these back to three to six inches with three or four buds each. During the summer remove faded flowers to force new blooms. So-called "ramblers" which bloom only in June should have all two-year-old canes cut to their source after flowering.

WINTER PROTECTION. In colder areas of the country, where temperatures fall regularly below zero, winter protection of bushes is necessary. Wait until after a killing frost (15° to 20°F), then bring in some soil and mound it up around the trunk of the bush to a height of six or seven inches. In spring, after the weather has warmed up and new growth commenced, remove the earth mound.

DRYING ROSES FOR CUT-FLOWER ARRANGEMENTS. You will not only want to use roses and rosebuds for live arrangements but in dried bouquets. The best way to dry whole miniature or standard rosebuds is to use the silica gel or oven or microwave drying methods (see pages 25–31). Rose material is particularly susceptible to insect infestation, so after drying be sure to follow the advice on storing the flowers with mothballs for several weeks.

Modern Roses

The most readily available roses are "modern" roses, many of which are suitable for the cut-flower garden. Of the hundreds of rose varieties available, the following offer both strong fragrance and vigorous growth. Vase life for all roses is from 3 to 7 days.

Hybrid Teas and Grandiflora

Hybrid teas are the best known, ranging in height from 2½ to 7 feet. Most are 3 to 5 feet tall

CULTIVAR	ROSE TYPE	COLOR
'Arizona'*	Grandiflora	Yellow-orange
'Chrysler Imperial'*	Hybrid tea	Red
'Command Performance'*	Hybrid tea	Orange
'Crimson Glory'*	Hybrid tea	Red
'Electron'*	Hybrid tea	Deep pink
'Fragrant Cloud'*	Hybrid tea	Red-orange
'Granada'*	Hybrid tea	Red-and-yellow
'Honor'	Hybrid tea	White
'Medallion'	Hybrid tea	Light apricot
'Mister Lincoln'*	Hybrid tea	Red
'Oklahoma'*	Hybrid tea	Red
'Ole'	Grandiflora	Red
'Peace'	Hybrid tea	Yellow-pink
'Perfume Delight'*	Hybrid tea	Cerise
'Pristine'	Hybrid tea	White with pink
'Queen Elizabeth'	Grandiflora	Pink
'Sheer Bliss'	Hybrid tea	Pinkish white
'Sterling Silver'*	Hybrid tea	Lavender
'Sundowner'*	Grandiflora	Red-orange
'Sutter's Gold'*	Hybrid tea	Yellow
'Tournament of Roses'	Grandiflora	Coral pink
'Tropicana'*	Hybrid tea	Red-orange
'Unforgettable'	Hybrid tea	Pink
'White Delight'	Hybrid tea	White-pink

'Pristine' is a particularly fragrant rose, always welcome in arrangements.

when dried. Here are some recommended varieties. Those marked with an asterisk bear the most fragrance.

CULTIVAR	COLOR
'Anabell'*	Orange-pink
'Angel Face'	Lavender
'Bahia'*	Coral-orange
'Cathedral'	Scarlet tinted salmon
'City of Belfast'	Red
'Class Act'	White
'Europeana'	Red
'Eutin'	Carmine-red
'First Kiss'*	Pink
'French Lace'	Ivory
'Ginger'	Scarlet-orange
'Gingersnap'	Bright orange
'Intrigue'	Red-purple
'Katherine Loker'	Yellow
'Merci'	Red
'Orangeade'	Orange
'Pleasure'	Coral-pink
'Red Pinocchio'	Red
'Showbiz'	Scarlet
'Spartan'	Orange
'Summer Fashion'	Pink-yellow
'Sun Flare'	Yellow
'Sunsprite'	Yellow
'Trumpeter'	Orange-red

and produce a single flower on a long stem. Some are fragrant, but many are not. Grandifloras are somewhat larger than the hybrid teas and are the result of a cross between hybrid teas and floribundas. These produce up to a half-dozen blooms on each stem. They are vigorous and most are fragrant. Those listed to the left are recommended for cut-flower use. Those marked with an asterisk bear the most fragrance.

Floribundas

These are small plants, two to four feet high, extremely vigorous, hardy, and disease resistant. They are usually covered with blossoms, smaller than those of hybrid teas or grandifloras. Although most bear some scent, yellow 'Sunsprite' is particularly fragrant and retains its bright yellow color

Climbers

Quantity of material is what you are looking for when you plan your cut-flower garden, so if you have the space, include a climber in your planting scheme as they offer extravagant bloom. The plants do not attach themselves to surfaces, but must be tied to trellises, fences, and other supports. Many

This old-fashioned single pale pink climber can be used to add delicate blooms to arrangements.

Miniatures

These are lilliputian versions of the larger varieties, growing to a mere one foot. If space is a problem, they are your best option. Minis offer tiny blossoms, which add enchanting touches to arrangements. These new mini floras (miniature floribundas) provide the most cutting material.

CULTIVAR	COLOR
'Classic Sunblaze'	Pink, (unlike its bigger pink sisters, this pink dries well)
'Orange Sunblaze'	Orange
'Red Sunblaze'	Bright red
'Royal Sunblaze'	Yellow with scarlet edges

grow from ten to twelve feet. Those marked with an asterisk bear the most fragrance.

These traditional miniatures do not offer as much cutting material per plant, but do offer a wide range of color.

CULTIVAR	COLOR
'America'*	Coral
'Blaze'	Bright red
'Climbing Chrysler Imperial'*	Red
'Climbing Crimson Glory'*	Red
'Climbing Sutter's Gold'*	Yellow
'Climbing Tropicana'	Red-orange
'Don Juan'*	Deep red
'Golden Showers'	Yellow
'New Dawn'	Pink, turning white in summer
'Royal Sunset'*	Orange

CULTIVAR	COLOR
'Beauty Secret'	Bright red
'Blizzard'	White
'Cartwheel'	Pink
'Charm Bracelet'	Gold
'Debut'	Deep red–white blend
'Paper Doll'	Apricot
'Puppy Love'	Multicolored orange, pink, and yellow
'Red Cascade'	Red
'Red Flush'	Red
'Rise 'n Shine'	Yellow
'Starina'	Orange-red
'Suzy Q'	Pink

Old-fashioned roses like the hybrid perpetual 'Hugh Dickson' are highly fragrant and once again in vogue with gardeners and flower arrangers.

Old-Fashioned Roses

The old-fashioned cabbage, damask, gallica, and alba roses, now enjoying a renewed popularity with gardeners, are the most heavily scented of all and thus add appealing fragrance to cut-flower arrangements. Their bloom is more profuse and the flowers more lush than those of most modern roses and they are often disease resistant, entailing less care.

However, they are not readily available in local garden centers and nurseries, but there are mail-order houses which specialize in them. If you wish to include some in your cutting garden, check the sources list at the back of the book and write for catalogs. These are usually very well-written and contain a great deal of descriptive and historical information about the varieties offered.

David Austin English Roses

These magnificent new hybrids are the culmination of nearly forty years of research and rose breeding by David C. H. Austin of Great Britain. The result of crossing old roses with modern bush roses, their form and flower, delicacy of coloring, and rich fragrance can be compared with those of the damask, gallica, and alba roses of the past. However, unlike these, they bloom repeatedly throughout the season.

You are unlikely to find these in local garden centers and nurseries. However, more and more mail-order houses are now offering them.

❧

10

Flowering and Evergreen
Shrubs and Trees

· · ·

Almost all properties include shrubs and trees in the landscape; however, few are planned with an eye to providing flowers, foliage, and berries for flower arrangements. But why not avail yourself of these generous plants?

There are shrubs and trees to fit into every landscape. Blooms come in every color of the rainbow, foliage ranges from feathery to leathery in every conceivable shade of green. And many sport brilliantly colored berries in the fall and winter. In short, there is a place for shrubs and flowering trees on everyone's property. Not only do they add great beauty to your landscape, they also provide you with an abundance of unusual material for arrangements throughout the year.

WHERE TO BUY. I've included shrubs and trees which are generally available throughout the country, if not at garden centers or nurseries, then through mail-order houses. Local garden centers or nurseries are often the best source for shrubs and flowering trees if you are starting out with your landscape scheme, as generally speaking, they offer only varieties which are recommended for your area. And, if the nursery is reliable and knows its business, it can also offer you all kinds of information about any special problems you might encounter with a particular variety, or any special planting instructions you will want to follow.

For mail-order shrubs and trees, write for catalogs early in the season, January or February at the

There are literally thousands of rhododendron varieties; however, those with small blossom clusters are perhaps the most appropriate for flower arrangements.

latest. When they arrive, study them carefully, along with the entries that follow, and make your selections. Be sure to check the USDA zones and order only those suitable for your location. When you've made your choices, it is a good idea to telephone your local cooperative extension service, usually listed in the phone book under county administration. Ask to speak to the agricultural division and tell them that you want advice on the species you've chosen. This is a free service offered all over the country and one which you pay for indirectly through your taxes. Then order your plants. Almost all mail-order nurseries ship at the proper planting time and include all instructions for immediate care, planting, and cultivation through the season.

WHERE TO PLANT. The planning of shrub and flowering tree plantings is considerably more complicated than installing bulbs, perennials, or annuals, this primarily because they are permanently installed. Once planted and grown to maturity, they require a great deal of effort to move, although some of the smaller species can be moved even after they've reached full size. Such moving should be done only in early spring or early fall. For our purposes here, consider your plans as permanent.

There are many ways to employ shrubs and flowering trees in the landscape. They can be used in foundation plantings, as hedges, in shrub borders along the sides, back, or front of your property, or in borders to divide one area of your property from another. If you mix deciduous

Flowering and Evergreen Shrubs and Trees

shrubs, dwarf conifers, and broad-leaved ever-greens, you can attain a planting which offers interest throughout the season. But, more to the point, if you select your plantings from those included here, you will have a bounty of cutting material for arrangements throughout the year.

SELECTING A SITE. As far as light requirements are concerned, most shrubs and trees can be planted in either full sun or partial shade, with some thriving in shade or deep shade as well. Consult the individual entries for specific recommendations. Although some species will thrive in areas with poor drainage, most prefer a reasonably well-drained location. To test a site for drainage, see the instructions on page 59.

PLANNING A PLANTING. As always, work it out on graph paper. Then, go outdoors to the area and try to visualize the planting. One way you can help yourself visualize the ultimate height of the various plants you wish to use is to insert bamboo sticks or poles measured to the mature height of the selected plant in the spot where the plant will grow.

Although it is only common sense to take note of the windows when planning a foundation planting, many people neglect to do so. Do not plant tall shrubs in front of windows, for they will block the view outside and prevent sunlight from shining into the house.

Also, consider the doorway. Avoid shrubs which will overgrow their bounds and impede passage to and from the house. Further, avoid planting shrubs which may have thorns on them close to the entrance of the house.

When you are ready to install your foundation or shrub border planting, take your chart with you to the garden for reference and bring a yardstick to properly measure distances.

PREPARING THE SOIL. Although many shrubs and trees are not particularly fussy about soil, it is a good idea to prepare the bed before installing the plants to create the proper growing conditions for the young plants and to give them a proper start in their new home. After you've selected the site for a particular plant, dig a hole about one and a half feet deep by three feet in diameter, this in accordance with the old rule of thumb, a five-dollar plant requires a ten-dollar hole. If the plant you have selected is acid-loving (these are usually the broad-leaved evergreens), mix the soil with organic matter such as sphagnum peat moss or well-rotted compost at a ratio of about one part soil to one part organic matter. If the plant does not require acid conditions, mix about one part organic matter to two parts soil. Return the mixture to the hole and water thoroughly. Do this about a week in advance of putting in your plants.

WHEN TO PLANT. Although early to midspring is the recommended time for most shrubs and trees, recent research shows that early fall is as good a time for most kinds, sometimes better. The reason for this is that young plants will not have to undergo the high temperatures of summer or prolonged dry spells. If you do install a fall planting, after the first heavy frost cover the entire planting with a six-inch layer of salt hay mulch to prevent the plants from heaving due to alternate freezing and thawing, thus possibly exposing surface roots to the elements. Check with your local garden center or nursery about the advisability of fall planting in your area and be sure that they offer a guarantee on any plants you purchase upon their recommendation.

PLANTING SHRUBS AND TREES. Once you've prepared the soil, dig a hole about twice as wide and deep as the rootball in the case of container or bagged-and-burlapped stock, and the same for the root structure of bare-root plants. Position the plant in the hole at the level at which it was grown at the nursery. On bare rootstock you can almost always see where the soil level was on the bark of the plant. Fill in soil beneath, around, and on top of the roots. Tamp down firmly, then water thoroughly. When the water has drained, tamp down and water thoroughly again. Keep in mind that very few shrubs and flowering trees require fertilizer at planting time if you have fortified the soil before doing so.

If you plant in the spring, mulch will help keep weeds down and retain moisture. And although many shrubs and trees are drought resistant, while they are establishing themselves in the earth during the first year, they require regular watering, particularly during summer drought. Beyond that, it is a good idea during prolonged periods of summer drought to water to a depth of 1½ feet at least once a week.

MAINTENANCE. Although most shrubs and flowering trees will survive and even thrive without an annual feeding, for best results, each spring before growth commences work about a cup of all-purpose 5-10-5 fertilizer into the soil around the plant. It is not necessary to deadhead (remove spent blossoms) from most shrubs and flowering trees, although both rhododendrons and deciduous azaleas provide a more resplendent display if the spent blossoms are removed each spring.

PESTS AND DISEASES. Most shrubs and flowering trees resist pest and disease infestation. These are the most common problems which may arise, though keep in mind it'll be unlikely you will have problems with them:

Powdery mildew. The leaves will become disfigured by a white fuzz. Spray with Captan or Benomyl according to the manufacturer's instructions from midsummer until early September to control this problem. Lilac is most susceptible.

Scale. These attach themselves to the undersides of the leaves of some broad-leaved evergreens and to the bark of some deciduous shrubs such as pussy willow. They suck the juices of the plant, and if not controlled, can eventually kill the plant. Dormant oil spray, available at garden centers and nur-

series, applied very early in the spring will smother them and control the problem.

Red spider. When this mite strikes plants become yellow and weak and the undersides of the leaves dirty-looking. Webs appear near the ribs or margins of leaves and then over the entire surface. If trouble is detected in its early stages, use Tedion; later stages require Kelthane, both available at garden centers and nurseries. Use according to the manufacturer's instructions.

Flowering Shrubs

Arrowwood
(Viburnum dentatum)

USDA zones: 3 to 9.
Color: White.
Description: Attractive flowers borne on deep

Viburnum dentatum *offers fragrant blooms in spring, lush green foliage all summer, and red berries in the fall.*

green foliage which turns bright red in the autumn. It bears blue berries, which begin to appear after flowering.

Height: 8 to 14′.

Soil: Almost any soil.

Light: Full sun or partial shade.

Moisture: Drought resistant once established, but water regularly during summer drought for best results.

Planting time: Spring or fall.

Bloom time: Mid- to late spring.

Length of bloom: 2 to 3 weeks.

Pruning; Little pruning required, but if necessary, prune in late fall after berries have fallen.

Forcing: No.

Live arrangements: Yes.

Vase life: 5 to 7 days.

Drying: No.

Tips: V. 'Doublefile' is a vigorous variety. Berries attract the birds.

Azalea (Deciduous) or Exbury, Ghent, or Mollis Azalea

USDA zones: 4 to 8, depending on variety.

Color: Brilliant red, purple, orange, yellow, pink, salmon, coral, white, or combinations thereof.

Description: Clustered blooms held on a loosely structured plant.

Height: 3 to 8′.

Soil: Rich, slightly acid.

Light: Full sun or partial shade.

Moisture: Plant will tell you if it needs watering by wilting visibly.

Planting time: Spring or fall, but will survive summer planting.

Bloom time: Mid- to late spring.

Length of bloom: 2 to 4 weeks.

Pruning: After spring blooming period.

Forcing: No.

Live arrangements: Yes.

Vase life: 5 to 7 days.

Drying: No.

Tips: Foliage tends to mildew during summer. Spray from early summer to fall with Captan or Benomyl fungicides according to the manufacturer's instructions if this bothers you. Azaleas certainly are among the most beautiful of all shrubs. Since deciduous azaleas require slightly acid soil, scratch in one tablespoon of Miracid around each plant in spring before blooming. Remove spent blooms to assure spectacular flowering the following year. Exbury and Knaphill hybrids are the best of the deciduous azaleas.

WARNING: *If you use this for indoor arrangements, keep in mind that all parts of the plant are poisonous to dogs, cats, and human beings if eaten, and can be fatal!*

Beautyberry
(Callicarpa bodinieri 'Profusion')

USDA zones: 5 to 7.

Color: Pale bluish.

Description: Small blossoms held over 2 to 5″ medium green leaves that are bronze when young; followed in fall by bright purple berries.

Height: 3 to 4′.

Soil: Ordinary.

Light: Full sun or partial shade.

Moisture: Drought resistant once established, but water regularly during summer drought for best results.

Planting time: Spring or fall.

Bloom time: Flowers in July and August; bears berries from mid- to late fall.

Length of bloom: Flowers from 2 to 3 weeks, berries up to 3 months.

Pruning: Late winter before buds show green.

Forcing: No.
Live arrangements: Yes, berries only.
Vase life: 1 to 2 weeks.
Drying: Yes. Hang dry berries in fall.
Tips: Unique because of its bright purple berries. Hard to come by, but worth the effort for unusual fall and dried arrangements. Niche Gardens offers this hard-to-find species (see Sources).

Bluebeard
(Caryopteris)

USDA zones: 6 to 11.
Color: Deep blue-purple.
Description: Many flowered clusters held along stems over feathery, pale green foliage.
Height: 3′.
Soil: Sandy loam.
Light: Full sun or partial shade.
Moisture: Drought resistant once established, but water regularly during summer drought for best results.
Planting time: Spring or fall.
Bloom time: Late summer to early fall.
Length of bloom: 4 to 6 weeks.
Pruning: Cut to 4″ in late winter.
Forcing: No.
Live arrangements: Yes.
Vase life: 5 to 7 days.
Drying: Yes. Hang dry or silica dry.
Tips: One of the few flowering shrubs that blooms at the end of the summer. Easy to grow, non-problematical. 'Dark Knight' is a favorite variety.

Bridal Wreath
(Spiraea prunifolia)

USDA zones: 4 to 8.
Color: White, pink, red.
Description: Graceful arching branches completely covered with flowers. Foliage is medium green.
Height: 5 to 6′.
Soil: Almost any soil.
Light: Full sun or partial shade.
Moisture: Drought resistant once established, but water regularly during summer drought for best results.
Planting time: Spring or fall.
Bloom time: Late spring.
Length of bloom: 2 to 3 weeks.
Pruning: After bloom period.
Forcing: Yes.
When to cut for forcing: Mid-March.
Live arrangements: Yes.
Vase life: 5 to 7 days.
Drying: No.
Tips: Prune in fall every few years to maintain vigor. Do this by removing branches at soil level, not by cutting branches halfway down. 'Vanhouteii', a fountain-shaped plant, is the most commonly planted variety. *S. japonica* 'Goldmount' forms a low mounded plant bearing pink flowers in May and golden leaves throughout the growing season. However, this is suitable only for cool climates, as the leaves sunburn badly in the South.

Burning Bush
(Euonymus alata compacta)

USDA zones: 3 to 8.
Color: Inconspicuous yellow flowers in spring followed by orange fruits, but is grown primarily for its brilliant red autumn foliage.
Description: Handsome, medium green foliage, es-

pecially attractive in winter because of its exposed decorative corky bark.

Height: Compact variety grows to 6'.
Soil: Almost any soil.
Light: Full sun or partial shade.
Moisture: Drought resistant once established, but water regularly during summer drought for best results.
Planting time: Spring or fall.
Pruning: In fall to encourage bushy growth.
Forcing: No.
Live arrangements: Yes.
Vase life: 5 to 7 days.
Drying: No.
Tips: Autumn foliage is spectacular both in the garden and in flower arrangements.

Deutzia, Pink
(Deutzia gracilis rosea)

USDA zones: 4 to 8.
Color: Delicate pink or white.
Description: Handsome, upright shrub with a profusion of 5-petaled blossoms on medium green foliage.
Height: 3'.
Soil: Almost any soil.
Light: Full sun or partial shade.
Moisture: Drought resistant once established, but water regularly during summer drought for best results.
Planting time: Spring or fall.
Bloom time: Late spring.
Length of bloom: 2 to 3 weeks.
Pruning: After blooming period.
Forcing: Yes.
When to cut for forcing: Mid-March.
Live arrangements: Yes.
Vase life: 3 to 5 days.
Drying: No.

Tips: Because of its tidy, low-growing tendency, deutzia is very useful in landscaping a small property. The profusion of bloom provides an abundance of cutting material. 'Pink-a-boo' is especially lovely.

Dogwood, Red-twig
(Cornus alba 'Sibirica')

USDA zones: 2 to 8.
Color: Creamy white or yellow.
Description: Bright green-leaved shrub, bearing white berry clusters, which are relished by birds, in fall. Twigs turn brilliant red in winter and are prized for this reason, as they are useful in winter flower arrangements.
Height: 10 to 12'.
Soil: Almost any soil.
Light: Full sun or partial shade.
Moisture: Water regularly during summer drought.
Planting time: Spring or fall.
Bloom time: Late winter to early spring.
Length of bloom: 3 to 4 weeks.
Pruning: Late winter.
Forcing: No.
Live arrangements: Yes.
Vase life: Twigs cut in winter last for months.
Drying: No.
Tips: 'Sibirica' is recommended because it is more compact and grows less rampant than other varieties.

Double Globeflower
(Kerria japonica pleniflora)

USDA zones: 5 to 8.
Color: Bright gold.
Description: Attractive buttonlike blossoms cover the plant in spring. The foliage is dark green, remaining attractive all during season.

Height: 3 to 5'.

Soil: Almost any soil.

Light: Full sun or partial shade.

Moisture: Drought resistant once established, but water regularly during summer drought for best results.

Planting time: Spring or fall.

Bloom time: Mid- to late spring.

Length of bloom: 3 to 4 weeks.

Pruning: After bloom period.

Forcing: No.

Live arrangements: Yes.

Vase life: 2 to 4 days.

Drying: No.

Tips: Each spring, prune off brown tips only. Plant is tidy, does not grow rampant, and rarely needs major pruning. Easy to maintain.

Forsythia
(Forsythia × intermedia)

USDA zones: 5 to 8.

Color: Yellow or cream-colored.

Description: Upright or weeping shrub, depending on variety, with a profusion of small, lily-shaped blossoms on bright green foliage.

Height: 6 to 8'.

Soil: Almost any soil.

Light: Full sun or partial shade.

Moisture: Drought resistant once established, but water regularly during summer drought for best results.

Planting time: Spring or fall.

Bloom time: Early spring.

Length of bloom: 2 to 3 weeks.

Pruning: After spring bloom.

Forcing: Yes, one of the best.

When to cut for forcing: Early January to mid-March.

Varieties recommended for forcing: 'Beatrix Farrand', 'Linwood Gold', and the so-called white

forsythia, *Abeliophyllum distichum*.

Live arrangements: Yes.

Vase life: 7 to 14 days.

Drying: No.

Tips: Avoid weeping types as they require annual pruning to keep them under control. Some use forsythia as a hedge, clipping it in early spring. Avoid doing this, as a twiggy plant, half-covered with flowers, is ugly. 'Northern Lights' is a variety recommended for Zones 3 and 4, and, although it is not outstanding in flower, it has bloomed heavily in tests at the University of Minnesota after winter temperatures of −30°F.

Lilac
(Syringa)

USDA zones: 3 to 8.

Color: Pink, white, lilac, blue, deep purple.

Description: The familiar clusters of florets are held on a medium green leafed plant.

Height: 5 to 20'.

Soil: Fertile, well-drained.

Light: Full sun or partial shade.

Moisture: Drought resistant once established.

Planting time: Spring or fall.

Bloom time: Mid-spring.

Length of bloom: 2 to 3 weeks.

Pruning: Remove spent flower heads immediately after bloom period. Remove suckers (small twigs that grow from bottom of plant) as they appear.

Forcing: Yes.

When to cut for forcing: Early March.

Live arrangements: Yes.

Vase life: 5 to 7 days.

Drying: No.

Tips: There are many hybrids available which grow to a manageable height. Persian lilac, with its deep purple blooms, grows to only 6' and is useful in a shrub border. Korean lilac, with pink blooms, grows to only 5′. Most varieties are too tall for borders, but can be used as screens or planted in a grove in the distant parts of the landscape. Leaves tend to host mildew during summer. If this bothers you, spray with Captan or Benomyl fungicide beginning in early summer, according to manufacturer's instructions. Deadhead flowers for more profuse bloom the following year.

Pussy Willow
(Salix discolor)

USDA zones: 2 to 9.
Color: Pinkish gray.
Description: The familiar catkins of pussy willows precede the green foliage.
Height: About 10′.
Soil: Any soil will do.
Light: Full sun or partial shade.
Moisture: Drought resistant once established.
Planting time: Spring or fall.
Bloom time: Early spring.
Length of bloom: 2 to 4 weeks.
Pruning: After bloom period.
Forcing: Yes, one of the best.
When to cut for forcing: February.
Live arrangements: Yes.
Vase life: 2 to 3 weeks.
Drying: Yes. Water dry.
Tips: Use for a screen or background planting. Very hardy plant. The French variety is a vast improvement on the common pussy willow, which is very subject to scale. If you already have the common variety on your property, spray in late winter with dormant oil spray according to the manufacturers's instructions to smother the scale. Other varieties are *S. gracilistyla* (rose-gold pussy willow) and *S. caprea* (French pink pussy willow or goat willow).

Quince, Japanese Scarlet
(Chaenomeles japonica)

USDA zones: 4 to 8.
Color: White, pink-and-white, pink, salmon, orange, or red.
Description: Single or double blossoms borne on a loosely structured plant. Some varieties sport thorns.
Height: 5 to 10′.
Soil: Sandy loam.
Light: Full sun or partial shade.
Moisture: Drought resistant once established, but water regularly during summer drought for best results.
Planting time: Spring or fall.
Bloom time: Early spring.
Length of bloom: 2 to 3 weeks.
Pruning: After bloom period and only if plant becomes leggy.
Forcing: Yes.
When to cut for forcing: February to mid-March.
Live arrangements: Yes.
Vase life: 6 to 10 days.
Drying: No.
Tips: Easy to grow, nonproblematical.

Rhododendron, Korean
(Rhododendron mucronulatum)

USDA zones: 4 to 7.
Color: Rose-purple or pink.
Description: Azalealike blossoms cover bare branches. Handsome, deep green, glossy foliage.
Height: 5 to 8′.
Soil: Well-drained, ordinary.
Light: Partial shade.
Moisture: Drought resistant once established.
Planting time: Spring or fall.
Bloom time: Early spring.

Length of bloom: 2 to 3 weeks.

Pruning: Rarely needs pruning, but if necessary, after bloom period.

Forcing: Yes.

When to cut for forcing: Late January to early February.

Live arrangements: Yes.

Vase life: 5 to 7 days.

Drying: No.

Tips: This rhododendron is one of the earliest-blooming shrubs, flowering in tandem with forsythia. Underplanted with daffodils the outdoor effect is lovely.

WARNING: *If you use this for indoor arrangements, keep in mind that all parts of the plant are poisonous to dogs, cats, and human beings if eaten, and can be fatal!*

Winterberry
(Ilex verticillata 'Nana')

USDA zones: 3 to 8.

Color: Red berries.

Description: Berries held on 1 to 3″ medium green leaves.

Height: 3′.

Soil: Moderately fertile, acidic.

Light: Full sun to semishade.

Moisture: Keep well-watered during summer drought.

Planting time: Early to late spring.

Berry time: Late fall through midwinter.

Pruning: If plant gets rangy, cut back almost to the ground in late winter.

Forcing: No.

Live arrangements: Yes.

Vase life: 3 to 4 weeks.

Drying: No.

Tips: In order for berries to set, both male and female plants should be planted. Birds relish the berries.

Witch Hazel
(Hamamelis)

USDA zones: 4 to 8, depending on variety.

Color: Yellow, bright red, or orange.

Description: Ribbonlike blossoms, often fragrant, appear before foliage, which turns brilliant red, orange and yellow in fall. Shrub has treelike appearance.

Height: Can grow 15 to 20′, but can be controlled by pruning.

Soil: Well-drained with some acidity.

Light: Partial shade.

Moisture: Water regularly during summer drought.

The brilliant red berries of Ilex verticulata 'Nana', a deciduous holly also called winterberry, are always welcome in holiday arrangements.

Planting time: Spring or fall.

Bloom time: Late winter to early spring.

Length of bloom: Erratic. Can be anywhere from 3 to 6 weeks depending on weather.

Pruning: After bloom period, prune from top to maintain desired height.

Forcing: Yes.

When to cut for forcing: January.

Live arrangements: Yes.

Vase life: 5 to 7 days.

Drying: No.

Tips: The earliest-blooming of all the flowering shrubs, witch hazel brightens the landscape as early as January during mild winters. They are particularly well-suited for growing under deciduous trees.

Flowering Trees

Crab Apple, Flowering
(Malus)

USDA zones: 4 to 8.

Color: White, pink to deep red, depending on cultivar.

Description: Blossoms precede deep green foliage which turns brilliant red in fall. Many varieties bear small red crab apples, varying in size from that of a berry to a small apple, in summer and fall. They are edible.

Height: Ultimately 25′.

Soil: Average.

Light: Full sun.

Moisture: Drought resistant once established, but water thoroughly during summer drought.

Planting time: Spring or fall.

Bloom time: Midspring.

Length of bloom: 2 to 4 weeks.

Pruning: Not usually necessary except to remove

damaged branches or to shape tree. Do this in late winter.

Forcing: Yes.

When to cut for forcing: Mid-March.

Live arrangements: Yes.

Vase life: 7 to 10 days.

Drying: No.

Tips: Dwarf and semidwarf varieties are suitable for use adjacent to patios and in small gardens. Standard-size trees can be used as specimen trees, in borders, or as backdrops. It is a good idea to check at a reliable local nursery for the names of varieties recommended for your particular area.

Dogwood, Flowering
(Cornus florida)

USDA zones: 5 to 9.

Color: White, pink, red.

Description: Blossoms are actually bracts, not flowers, and appear before the handsome deep green foliage leafs out. Fall color is brilliant red to purple, with red berries which attract birds. Horizontal branching pattern.

Height: Ultimately 25 to 30′.

Soil: Average.

Light: Full sun or partial shade.

Moisture: Drought resistant once established but water regularly during summer drought.

Planting time: Spring or fall.

Bloom time: Midspring.

Length of bloom: 3 to 4 weeks.

Pruning: Not necessary except to remove damaged or dead limbs.

Forcing: Yes.

When to cut for forcing: Mid-March.

Live arrangements: Yes.

Vase life: 8 to 10 days.

Drying: No.

Tips: 'White Cloud' and 'Cherokee', a red variety,

are recommended. Unfortunately, this lovely American species is now being attacked by a disease called anthracnose. Older specimens are the most vulnerable. Water thoroughly and regularly during the growing season to avoid stressing the plant and making it vulnerable to disease. If leaves curl and dry, and the branch looks dead, remove the branch with pruning shears at once, dispose of it in the garbage or burn it, and sterilize the shears with rubbing alcohol or household bleach before using again. Spraying regularly with a fungicide such as Captan or Benlate according to the manufacturer's instructions may help. One species, *C. kousa*, also called Japanese dogwood (zones 6 to 9), is not susceptible to the disease. Although not a spring bloomer, and thus not suitable for forcing, this variety sports white bracts which appear in summer, with orange and red autumn foliage, and small strawberrylike red inedible fruit. I particularly recommend the variety "Summer Stars'.

Magnolia, Saucer
(Magnolia × soulangiana)

USDA zones: 4 to 11.
Color: White, pink, purplish red.
Description: Chalice-shaped, six-inch flowers followed by medium-green, oval, velvety foliage. Deciduous with gray bark which is attractive during the winter.
Height: Ultimately 25'.
Soil: Average.
Light: Full sun.
Moisture: Drought resistant once established, but water thoroughly during summer drought.
Planting time: Spring or fall.
Bloom time: Midspring.
Length of bloom: 2 to 3 weeks.
Pruning: Not usually necessary except to remove

damaged limbs. Do this in late winter.
Forcing: Yes.
When to cut for forcing: February.
Live arrangements: Yes.
Vase life: 2 to 4 days.
Drying: No.
Tips: In zones 6 to 8 it is best not to plant this species in a spot with southern exposure, as late frosts can discolor blossoms forced into bloom by this protected environment. Eastern, western, or northern exposures are preferable. In zones 4 and 5, southern exposure is fine.

Prunus × blireiana, P. persica, P. sieboldii

USDA zones: Vary according to species. Check locally.
Color: White, pink, fuchsia.
Description: All sport spectacular spring blooms but most are fruitless, therefore eliminating maintenance, pest and disease control, fruit drop, and other complications of fruit trees. *P. sieboldii* (flowering cherry) has single or double blossoms in white or pink, some in pendant clusters. The bark is a lustrous mahogany when young, similar in appearance to that of birch. *P. x blireiana* (flowering plum) carries smaller blossoms in white or pink. Many are purple-leaved, with some bearing red or coppery red coloration. Some produce a small fruit which can be a nuisance if planted near a walk or patio. Although *P. persica* (flowering peach) is very beautiful, it is subject to many of the pests and diseases of its fruit-bearing cousins, requiring considerable maintenance and therefore is generally not recomended for the average home planting.
Height: Most grow to 20', some to 40'.
Soil: Average.
Light: Full sun.

The cascading flowering branches of this weeping cherry tree create interesting lines in arrangements.

Moisture: Drought resistant when established, but water thoroughly during summer drought.

Planting time: Spring or fall.

Bloom time: All bloom in midspring.

Length of bloom: 2 to 3 weeks.

Pruning: Not usually necessary, except to remove damaged limbs. Do this in late winter.

Forcing: Yes.

When to cut for forcing: P. × *blireiana*, late January; *P. persica*, late January; *P. sieboldii*, late January to mid-March.

Live arrangements: Yes.

Vase life: 7 to 14 days.

Drying: No.

Tips: The selection of cultivars is vast, so it is perhaps best to consult with a local nursery or with your local Cooperative Extension for varieties recommended for your area.

WARNING: *If you use* P. sieboldii *for indoor arrangements, keep in mind that twigs and foliage of the plant are poisonous to dogs, cats, and human beings if eaten, and can be fatal!*

Rowan or European Mountain Ash
(Sorbus aucuparia)

USDA zones: 3 to 7.

Color: White.

Description: Small blossoms cover the tree in spring, hanging clusters of orange or red berries in fall. Leaves are small and oval, turning to yellow or orange-red in fall.

Height: Larger varieties grow to 50′; however, the smaller American ash *(S. americana)* grows to around 15′ and is well suited to the average landscape.

Soil: Average.

Light: Full sun.

Moisture: Drought resistant once established.

Planting time: Spring or fall.

Bloom time: Flowers in midspring, berries in early to late fall.

Length of bloom: Berries hold for 4 to 6 weeks.

Pruning: Not usually necessary, except to remove damaged limbs. Do this in late winter.

Forcing: No.

Live arrangements: Yes, but only with berries.

Vase life: 7 to 14 days.

Drying: No.

Tips: Especially attractive when planted in front of evergreens which set off the berries during fall and winter.

Broad-leaved Evergreens
Azalea and Rhododendron

USDA zones: 3 to 11, depending on variety.

Color: The full range of colors.

Description: Large and small clusters of florets on handsome deep green foliage.

Height: 1 to 40′.

Soil: Rich soil on the acid side.

Light: Full sun or partial shade.

Moisture: Keep well-watered during summer drought.

Planting time: Spring or fall.

Bloom time: Mid- to late spring, depending on variety.

Length of bloom: 3 to 4 weeks.

Forcing: Yes.

When to cut for forcing: January and February.

Live arrangements: Yes.

Vase life: 7 to 10 days.

Drying: No.

Tips: These are an entire world of their own. Inquire locally as to which varieties are best for your area. They combine especially well with spring-flowering bulbs.

WARNING: *If you use these for indoor arrangements, keep in mind that all parts of the plant are poisonous to dogs, cats, and human beings if eaten and can be fatal!*

Boxwood, Japanese
(Buxus microphylla)

USDA zones: 6 to 9.

Color: No blossoms.

Description: Attractive, small round-tipped leaves. Some varieties sport white or black berries in fall.

Height: 1 to 3′.

Soil: Average, loamy soil.

Light: Full sun or partial shade.

Moisture: Keep well-watered during summer drought.

Planting time: Spring or fall.

Pruning: Not necessary except to remove damaged limbs. Do this in late winter.

Forcing: No.

Live arrangements: Yes, greenery useful.

Vase life: 1 to 3 weeks.

Drying: No.

Tips: Provides long-lasting greenery in arrangements.

WARNING: *If you use this for indoor arrangements, keep in mind that all parts of the plant are poisonous to dogs, cats, and human beings if eaten, and can be fatal!*

Camellia

USDA zones: 7 to 11.

Color: Red, pink, white, or combinations thereof.

Description: Spectacular 3-inch blooms set on handsome deep green foliage.

Height: C. japonica (common camellia) 10 to 15′; C. sasanqua, 12′.

Soil: Rich loam, so fortify at planting time with substantial quantitites of rotted compost or sphagnum peat moss at a ratio of about one part additive to one part soil.

Light: For best results, plant in partial shade, although plant will survive in full sun.

Moisture: Keep well-watered during summer drought.

Planting time: Spring or fall.

Bloom time: C. japonica, late winter to early spring, depending on location; C. sasanqua, early to late fall.

Length of bloom: 3 to 4 weeks.

Pruning: Not necessary except to remove damaged limbs. Do this in late winter.

Forcing: No.

Live arrangements: Yes. Although they have no scent, camellias are so very beautiful in arrangements. Or you can simply float them in a large bowl filled with water. At dinner, place some small candles amid the floating blossoms for a particularly dramatic effect.

Vase life: 3 to 6 days.

Drying: No.

Tips: Camellias are much more hardy than generally thought. Although most people think they grow only in the South, they will thrive in protected areas of Zone 6, although a very severe winter may kill all the foliage. In Zone 7 where I live, camellias grow and although two severe winters during the 1970s did kill the foliage to the ground, the plant survived and is now about ten feet tall. Because full sun tends to burn and brown blossoms in early spring, a southern exposure is not the best location to plant camellias. Eastern or even northern exposure is preferred. They are particularly dramatic espaliered against a wall.

Euonymous japonica 'Marginata'

USDA zones: 7 to 8.

Color: Insignificant white blossoms in spring and insignificant red berries in fall.

Description: Glossy, wide, yellow margins on green foliage.

Height: 4' at maturity.

Soil: Ordinary.

Light: Full sun or partial shade.

Moisture: Keep well-watered during summer drought.

Planting time: Spring or fall.

Pruning: Only to maintain desired height.

Variegated euonymus can be used to add variety to any foliage-enhanced arrangement.

The Cut-flower Garden

Forcing: No.
Live arrangements: Yes.
Vase life: 1 to 3 weeks.
Drying: No.
Tips: Useful in stylized arrangements because of its yellow foliage.

Fire Thorn, Scarlet
(Pyracantha coccinea)

USDA zones: 6 to 9.
Color: White.
Description: Clusters of blossoms followed by abundant, showy inedible clusters of red or orange berries. Small leaves may fall late in the season in northern parts of growing range.
Height: Can grow to 20', or can be contained and espaliered against walls.
Soil: Not fussy.
Light: Full sun or partial shade.
Moisture: Keep well-watered during summer drought.
Planting time: Spring or fall.
Bloom time: Early summer flowers, berries in fall and winter.
Length of bloom: 2 to 3 weeks.
Pruning: Usually necessary only to keep a vigorous specimen in bounds. Do this in late fall and use cuttings for arrangements.
Forcing: No.
Live arrangements: Yes.
Vase life: 1 to 2 weeks.
Drying: No.
Tips: 'Lalandei' has been found to be hardy as far north as Minneapolis. In the garden it is a splendid plant for autumn and winter berry color. In autumn arrangements its brilliant orange color works well with dried grasses and autumn chrysanthemums. Use it in combination with holly during the holidays.

Holly, American
(Ilex opaca)

USDA zones: 5 to 8.
Color: Grown for red berries.
Description: Dark green, lustrous spiny leaves, bearing fruit in the fall.
Height: Can grow to 50', but can be kept in bounds by pruning.
Soil: Sandy loam.
Light: Full sun.
Moisture: Keep well-watered during summer drought.
Planting time: Spring only.
Pruning: Usually necessary only to keep a vigorous specimen in bounds. Do this in December and use cuttings for holiday decorating.
Forcing: No.
Live arrangements: Yes.
Vase life: 2 to 3 weeks.
Drying: No.
Tips: Used as a substitute for English holly in areas too cold for that species. Ideal for trimming the house at Christmas.

Holly, English
(Ilex aquifolium)

USDA zones: 6 to 9.
Color: Inconspicuous blossoms.
Description: Glossy green or blue-green foliage, bearing red, white, or orange berries.
Height: Can grow to 40', but can be kept in bounds by yearly pruning.
Soil: Sandy loam.
Light: Full sun.
Moisture: Keep well-watered during summer drought.
Planting time: Spring only.

This garden of dwarf conifers and grasses at the Dennis Di Traglia–Anthony Musto residence in Southold, New York, designed by Connie Cross of Cutchogue, New York, provides a bonanza of cutting material for late fall and winter arrangements.

Bloom time: Grown for foliage and fall and winter berries.

Pruning: Usually necessary only to keep a vigorous specimen in bounds. Do this in December and use cuttings for holiday decorations.

Forcing: No.

Live arrangements: Yes.

Vase life: 2 to 3 weeks.

Drying: No.

Tips: The classic Christmas greenery to "deck the halls." You simply can't have enough of this in your house during the holidays.

Dwarf Conifers

What would the holiday season be without some fresh evergreen foliage for decorating here and there about the house. Standard evergreen trees, although magnificent when fully grown, are almost always far too large for the average contemporary landscape. But you have an option, and a very satisfactory one. Because of the demand for smaller, more manageable varieties of evergreens, an entire world of dwarf conifers is now readily available at most garden centers and nurseries. Twenty-five years ago this was not the case. These dwarf beauties can be used in so many ways in the landscape and, for our purposes, provide coveted greenery to use for arrangements, wreaths, swags, and so forth in the home.

Although I've included a reasonable selection here, there are many more available through mail-order or even at your local garden center or nursery. Since most of these varieties thrive in most areas of the country, recommended USDA zones are not included.

Arborvitae, American
(Thuja occidentalis)

Description: Available in many shapes—pyramidal, conical, globular, columnar—in gold, and light to dark green voliage, depending on variety.
Soil: Ordinary.
Light: Full sun or partial shade.
Moisture: Drought resistant once established, but water regularly during summer drought.
Planting time: Spring or fall.
Recommended varieties:

- 'Emerald'. Narrow pyramidal form, emerald green foliage.
- 'Holmstrup'. Conical form, apple green foliage.
- 'Little Giant'. Globe form, rich green foliage.
- 'Nigra'. Conical form, dark green foliage.
- 'Rheingold'. Globe form, golden yellow foliage that deepens to copper-gold in winter.

False Cypress
(Chamaecyparis)

Description: Globular, pyramidal, or spreading, in silver-blue, green, or gold foliage, depending on variety.
Soil: Ordinary.
Light: Full sun or partial shade.
Moisture: Drought resistant once established, but water regularly during summer drought.
Planting time: Spring or fall.

Specimens such as this false cypress (Chamaecyparis obtusa lutea 'Nana') at Ed Rezek's "museum of dwarf conifers" in Malverne, New York, not only add elegance to the landscape, but offer cutting material for arrangements all during the year.

Recommended varieties: *C. obtusa nana*: Flat-topped form of Hinoki cypress with dark green foliage that turns bronze in winter; *C. o. gracilis*: Deep green foliage, upright growth; *C. obtusa* 'Aurea Nana' (Gold dwarf Hinoki cypress): Heavy-textured gold foliage; *C. o.* 'Kosteri': Lacy lustrous green foliage with broad growth habit; *C. obtusa* 'Torulosa' (Dwarf twisted branch cypress): Red-barked branches are twisted and filamented with dark green foliage, growing compactly into an irregular pyramidal form; *C. pisifera* 'Aurea Pendula' (Dwarf gold thread cypress): Low, compact with bright golden pendulous filaments; *C. p. filifera* 'Aurea Variegata Nana' (Dwarf gold-variegated cypress): Gold-variegated foliage; *C. p.* 'Argentea Nana' (Dwarf silver cypress): *C. pisifera* 'Argentea Variegata Nana' (Variegated dwarf silver threadleaf cypress): Silvery variegated foliage; Dense globe of soft-plumed silvery blue foliage; *C. p.* 'Sulphuria Nana' (Dwarf sulfur cypress): Broad mound of bright sulfur-colored foliage; *C. p.* 'Minima' (Dwarf threadleaf cypress): Compact growth with green foliage; *C. lawsoniana* 'Fletcheri' (Fletcher cypress): Narrow, columnar habit with green foliage; *C. nootkatensis* 'Pendula' (Weeping Nootka cypress): Branchlets of gray-green foliage hang vertically in long graceful streamers.

ing juniper): Blue foliage, with a creeping habit; *J. chinensis* 'Blue Vase': Grows to about 5', vase-shaped with blue foliage; *J. chinensis* 'Pfitzerana Aurea' (Gold tip juniper): Gray-green foliage with bright golden color on new growth in spring and summer; *J. procumbens nana* (Dwarf Japanese juniper): Short, stiff branches forming a bluish green carpet up to 6' across, mounding to 10" in the center; *J. japonica* 'Compacta' (Japanese juniper): Semiupright in habit, foliage slate to green shades; *J. rigida pendula* (Weeping needle juniper): Narrrow, tall, and pendant in habit, with blue-green foliage.

❧

Juniper
(*Juniperus*)

Description: Creeping, low and spreading, vase-shaped, or columnar, with varying shades of green-, blue-, or gold-needled foliage.
Soil: Ordinary.
Light: Prefers full sun, but will grow in partial shade.
Moisture: Drought resistant.
Planting time: Spring or fall.
Recommended varieties: *J. horizontalis* 'Plumosa' (Andorra juniper): Low, spreading habit, summer foliage silvery green, turning purple after frost; *J. h.* 'Bar Harbor': Low, creeping steel blue foliage with a fernlike appearance; *J. h.* 'Blue Chip': Silvery blue foliage, with a spreading, low-mounding habit; *J. h.* 'Glauca' (Blue creep-

Pine
(*Pinus*)

Description: Mound-shaped, columnar, pendulous, or conical with needled foliage in various shades of green and blue-green.
Soil: Ordinary.
Light: Full sun or partial shade.
Moisture: Drought resistant once established, but water regularly during summer drought.
Planting time: Spring or fall.
Recommended varieties: *P. strobus* 'Nana' (Dwarf Eastern white pine): Spreading habit with irregularly shaped silvery blue-green needles; *P. sylvestris* 'Glauca Nana' (Dwarf Scotch pine): Compact, slow-growing form of Scotch pine, conical when young becoming rounded with age, bearing blue-green needles; *P. pumila* (Dwarf Siberian stone pine): Spreading habit with light blue-green to blue needles.

Spruce
(Picea)

Description: Mounded, conical, pendulous, or columnar forms of blue- or green-needled foliage.

Soil: Ordinary.

Light: Full sun or partial shade.

Moisture: Drought resistant once established, but water regularly during summer drought.

Planting time: Spring or fall.

Recommended varieties: P. 'Alberta': Conical with medium green needles; *P. pungens* (Dwarf blue spruce): Conical with blue needles; *P. pungens globosa* (Dwarf globe blue spruce): Globe-shaped with silvery blue needles; *P. mariana nana* (Nest black spruce): Mound-shaped with short, light gray-green needles.

Yew
(Taxus)

Description: Medium to deep green needles on columnar, moundlike, or globular plants.

Soil: Ordinary.

Light: Full sun or partial shade.

Moisture: Drought resistant once established, but water regularly during summer drought.

Planting time: Spring or fall.

Recommended varieties: *T. brown*: Compact, dense mound-shaped with bright green needles. New spring growth is tinged with yellow at tips; *T. densiformis* (Spreading Japanese yew): Mound-shaped with medium green needles; *T.* 'Fairview': Globular and compact in growth with deep green needles.

Appendix A
Bloom Sequence Charts

· · ·

Annual Bloom Sequence
Early Spring

Pansy (*Viola* × *wittrockiana*): Early spring to early summer

Early Summer

Coreopsis or Calliopsis: Early summer to killing frost

Cornflower or bachelor's button *(Centaurea cyanus)*: Early to late summer

Cosmos: Early summer to killing frost

Dusty miller *(Senecio maritima)*: Early summer to killing frost

Marigold *(Tagetes)*: Early summer to killing frost

Marigold, pot *(Calendula officinalis)*: Early summer to killing frost

Snapdragon *(Antirrhinum)*: Early summer to killing frost and beyond

Spider plant *(Cleome)*: Early summer to killing frost

Midsummer

Cockscomb *(Celosia plumosa/cristata)*: Midsummer to killing frost

Forget-me-not *(Myosotis sylvatica)*: Late spring through early summer

Heliotrope: Midsummer to killing frost

Larkspur or annual delphinium *(Consolida ambigua,* syn. *Delphinium ajacis)*: Midsummer

Pincushion flower *(Scabiosa)*: Midsummer to killing frost

Pinks *(Dianthus chinensis)* and carnations *(D. caryophyllus)*: Midsummer to killing frost

Sage *(Salvia)*: Midsummer to killing frost

Zinnia: Midsummer to killing frost

Everlasting Bloom Sequence
Early Summer to Killing Frost

Bells of Ireland *(Moluccella laevis)*

Globe amaranth *(Gomphrena)*

Statice *(Limonium)*
Strawflower *(Helichrysum)*

Late Summer

Honesty or money plant *(Lunaria)*: Late summer to killing frost and beyond
Chinese lantern *(Physalis solanaceae)*: Early fall to killing frost and beyond

Perennial Bloom Sequence
Late Winter

Hellebore *(Helleborus)*: Late winter to early spring

Midspring

Bleeding heart *(Dicentra)*
Cushion spurge *(Euphorbia epithymoides)*
Violet *(Viola odorata)*: Mid- to late spring

Late Spring

Astilbe: Late spring to early summer
Campanula: Late spring to late summer
Clematis: Late spring to late fall
Coreopsis *(C. grandiflora/lanceolata)*: Late spring to killing frost
Delphinium: Late spring to early summer
Ferns: Late spring to late fall
Foxglove *(Digitalis grandiflora)*: Late spring
Goatsbeard *(Aruncus)*: Late spring
Iris, Bearded or German: Late spring to early summer
Iris, Siberian *(Iris sibirica)*: Late spring
Lupine *(Lupinus)*: Late spring to early summer
Peony *(Paeonia)*: Late spring
Pinks, garden *(Dianthus × alwoodii* and many others): Late spring and again in early fall

Poppy, oriental *(Papaver orientale)*: Late spring
Roses: Late spring to late fall
Sweet William *(Dianthus barbatus)*: Late spring to early summer
Wisteria, Japanese/Chinese *(Wisteria floribunda/sinensis)*: Late spring to early summer

Early Summer

Coneflower, purple *(Echinacea)*: Early summer to killing frost and beyond
Daisy, shasta *(Chrysanthemum × superbum)*: Early to late summer
Daisy, Transvaal *(Gerbera)*: Early summer to killing frost
Gayfeather *(Liatris)*: Early to midsummer
Grasses: Early summer to killing frost and beyond
Herbs (foliage types): Early summer to killing frost and beyond
Hosta: Early to late summer
Lady's mantle *(Alchemilla mollis)*: Early summer
Phlox *(Phlox carolina/paniculata)*: Early summer to late fall
Rose campion *(Lychnis coronaria)*: Early summer to early fall
Yarrow *(Achillea)*: Early summer to late fall

Midsummer

Baby's breath *(Gypsophila paniculata, G. repens rosea)*: Mid- to late summer
Blanketflower *(Gaillardia)*: Midsummer to late fall
Feverfew *(Chrysanthemum parthenium)*: Mid- to late summer
Lavender *(Lavandula)*: Midsummer to early fall
Sedum 'Autumn Joy': Midsummer to killing frost

Late Summer

Anemone, Japanese (*Anemone hupehensis japonica*): Late summer to early fall

Daisy, Michaelmas *(Aster)*: Late summer to killing frost and beyond

Early Fall

Chrysanthemum: Early fall to killing frost and beyond

Flowering and Fruit-bearing Shrub Bloom Sequence
Late Winter

Dogwood, red-twig (*Cornus alba* 'Sibirica'): Late winter to early spring

Witch hazel *(Hamamelis)*: Late winter to early spring

Early Spring

Forsythia × *intermedia*

Magnolia, star *(Magnolia stellata)*

Pussy willow *(Salix discolor)*

Quince, Japanese scarlet *(Chaenomeles japonica)*

Rhododendron, Korean *(Rhododendron mucronulatum)*

Midspring

Arrowwood *(Viburnum dentatum)*: Mid- to late spring

Azalea, Deciduous (or Exbury, Ghent, or Mollis azaleas): Mid- to late spring

Double globeflower *(Kerria japonica pleniflora)*: Mid- to late spring

Lilac *(Syringa)*: Midspring

Late Spring

Bridal wreath *(Spiraea prunifolia)*

Deutzia, pink *(Deutzia gracilis rosea)*

Late Summer

Bluebeard *(Caryopteris)*: Late summer to early fall

Midfall

Beautyberry (*Callicarpa bodinieri* 'Profusion'): Berries in mid- to late fall

Burning bush *(Euonymus alata compacta)*: Mid- to late fall

Late Fall

Winterberry (*Ilex verticillata* 'Nana'): Berries in late fall to midwinter

Flowering and Fruit-bearing Tree Bloom Sequence
Midspring

Cherry, flowering *(Prunus sieboldii)*

Crab apple, flowering *(Malus)*

Dogwood, flowering *(Cornus florida)*

Magnolia, saucer *(Magnolia* × *soulangiana)*

Peach, flowering *(Prunus persica)*

Plum, flowering *(Prunus triloba)*

Early Fall

Rowan or European mountain ash *(Sorbus aucuparia)*: Berries in early to late fall

Broad-Leaved Evergreen Bloom and Fruiting Sequence
Late Winter

Camellia japonica: Late winter to early spring

Midspring

Azalea and rhododendron: Mid- to late spring

Early Fall

Camellia sasanqua: Early to late fall

Fire thorn, scarlet *(Pyracantha coccinea)*: Berries in early to late fall and beyond

Holly, American *(Ilex opaca)*: Berries in early to late fall and beyond

Holly, English *(Ilex aquifolium)*: Berries in early to late fall and beyond

Appendix B
USDA Hardiness Zone Map

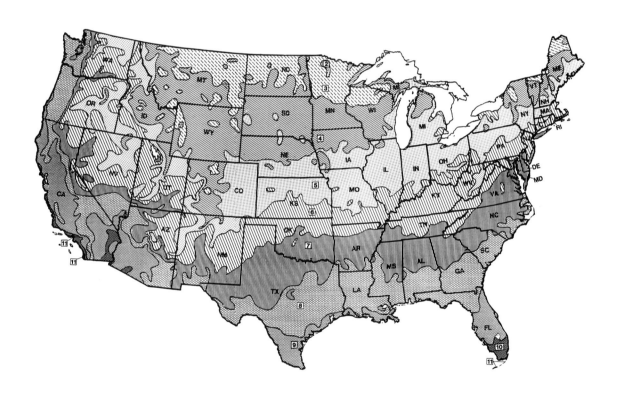

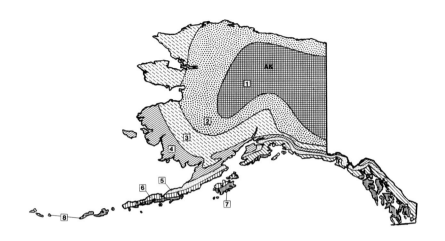

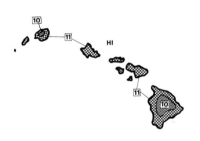

RANGE OF AVERAGE ANNUAL MINIMUM TEMPERATURES FOR EACH ZONE		
ZONE 1	BELOW −50° F	
ZONE 2	−50° TO −40°	
ZONE 3	−40° TO −30°	
ZONE 4	−30° TO −20°	
ZONE 5	−20° TO −10°	
ZONE 6	−10° TO 0°	
ZONE 7	0° TO 10°	
ZONE 8	10° TO 20°	
ZONE 9	20° TO 30°	
ZONE 10	30° TO 40°	
ZONE 11	ABOVE 40°	

USDA Hardiness Zone Map

Appendix C
Mail-order Sources

For Bulbs

Daffodil Mart, Brent & Becky Heath, Rt. 3, Box 7994, Gloucester, VA 23061. Phone: (804) 693-3966.
For the daffodil enthusiast or hobbyist, a wide selection of hard-to-find daffodils is offered here.

Smith & Hawken, 25 Corte Madera, Mill Valley, CA 94941. Phone: (415) 383-2000.
Only recently, this fine mail-order house has begun to offer bulbs. Some hard-to-find varieties are offered.

Van Bourgondien Bros., Box A, 245 Farmingdale Road, Rt. 109, Babylon, NY 11702. Phone: (800) 873-9444 outside New York; (800) 284-9333 in New York only.
The largest selection of bulbs available in the United States and the prices are very reasonable.

For Perennial Plants, Shrubs, and/or Trees

Bluestone Perennials, 7211 Middle Ridge Road, Madison, OH 44057. Phone: (800) 852-5243.
One of the best sources for perennial plants at very reasonable prices. These are small plants, available in either three- or six-packs. All plants are guaranteed to reach you in good condition and to grow. If they do not, the company will reship immediately or refund your money if you are not satisfied. They have recently added shrub varieties to their offerings.

Klehm Nursery, Box 197, Penny Road, Route 5, South Barrington, IL 60010-9555. Phone: (800) 553-3715.
A specialty house offering exceptionally beautiful and hard-to-find varieties of peonies, tree peonies, iris, hostas, ornamental grasses, and perennials.

Monrovia Nursery Co., 18331 E. Foothill Boulevard, Azusa, CA 91702-1336.
Although a wholesaler, better nurseries and garden centers usually carry their offerings. Ask your nurseryman to show you their catalog and then order anything special you want through the nursery.

Musser Forest, Inc., Route 119 North, Box 340, Indiana, PA 15710-0340. Phone: (412) 465-5685.
This house offers an extensive list of shrubs, deciduous flowering trees, dwarf conifers, and deciduous trees at very reasonable prices.

Niche Gardens, Department CF, 1111 Dawson Road, Chapel Hill, NC 27516. Phone: (919) 967-0078. Catalog costs $3.
Among the many unusual offerings of this house is the hard-to-find beautyberry (Callicarpa).

White Flower Farm, Litchfield CT, 06759-0050. Phone: (800) 944-9624.
Fine offerings of unusual and hard-to-find bulbs, shrubs, perennials, and flowering trees. Somewhat pricey, but plants are large and ready to set into a permanent place in the garden.

For Annual and Perennial Seeds

Thompson & Morgan, Box 1308, Jackson, NJ 08527. Phone: (800) 344-1500.
This house offers the most extensive list of perennial and annual seeds in the country, many of which are unavailable anywhere but here. It is well worth calling for their catalog to see their selection.

Park Seed Co., Cokesbury Road, Greenwood, SC 29647-0001. Phone: (800) 845-3366.
An extensive variety of annual and perennial seeds is available here.

W. Atlee Burpee Co., 300 Park Avenue, Warminster, PA 18974. Phone: (215) 674-4900.
Another house that offers a great variety of annual and perennial seeds.

For Roses

Jackson & Perkins Co., Box 1028, Medford, OR 97501. Phone: (800) 292-GROW.
America's largest purveyor of roses, now featuring the new David Austin English roses as well as all of the other traditional types and a selection of perennials, shrubs, and bulbs.

Roses of Yesterday and Today, 802 Brown's Valley Road, Watsonville, CA 95076.
This house offers a comprehensive selection of old-fashioned roses and some difficult-to-find modern roses.

For Seed Starting Kits

Gardener's Supply Co., 128 Intervale Road, Burlington, VT 05401. Phone: (800) 863-1700.
Their APS seed-starting kits are highly satisfactory for starting seeds under lights.

Index

. . .

Numerals in *italics* indicate illustrations.

Index

Index

Index